LANCASHIRE

· 1939-1945 ·

The Secret War

Ron Freethy

COUNTRYSIDE BOOKS
NEWBURY BERKSHIRE

COUNTRYSIDE BOOKS
3 Catherine Road
Newbury, Berkshire

To view our complete range of books,
please visit us at
www.countrysidebooks.co.uk

ISBN 978 1 85306 933 8

Designed by Peter Davies

Produced through MRM Associates Ltd., Reading
Typeset by CJWT Solutions, St Helens
Printed by Information Press, Oxford

Contents

COUNTY MAP OF LANCASHIRE
1939-1945

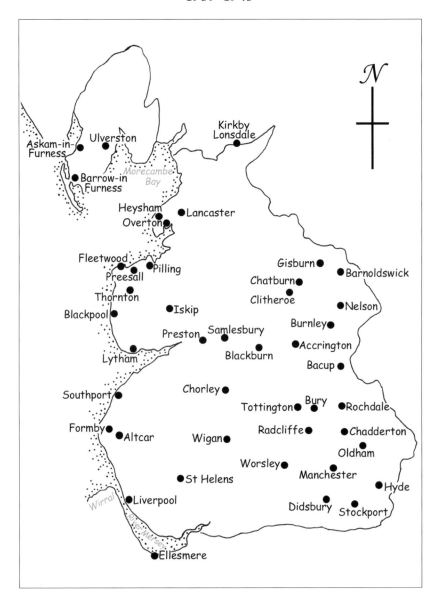

Acknowledgements

When I first began to research this book, I contacted local newspapers and their readers readily responded; I received more than 400 letters. Each has either been mentioned in the text or has been set aside for a subsequent volume. Local radio stations extended an equally welcoming response.

Some museums have been particularly helpful and none more so than the splendid Police Museum on Newton Street, in Manchester. Here, ex-policeman, Dennis Wood, and the curator, Duncan Broady, have both been a mine of information, especially with regard to my search for photographs. Simon Heyhow, the curator of Fleetwood Museum, opened his extensive archives relating to trawlers and the ICI chemical works, as did Stephen Bull of the Lancashire Museum at Preston, which has a gallery devoted to the Second World War. When faced with answering specific questions, such curators are seen in their very best light.

Bryn Tresatheric and the staff of the Dock Museum at Barrow-in-Furness were also generous with their time and resources. Books such as this should hopefully inspire people to visit these museums, which are goldmines for those quarrying for information about this period. Bryn Tresatheric's own book, *Barrow's Home Front 1939–45*, is a classic of its type but now sadly out of print.

I am also grateful to Dr Barry White, the John Rylands Librarian at the University of Manchester, for sourcing material relating to the Differential Analyser, designed by Douglas Hartree. Similarly, the staff at the Bidston Observatory opened up to me their archives relating to the Tidal Prediction Machine. They unearthed material that I thought had been lost forever. Keith Hall, of Castle Cement at Clitheroe, also provided me with archive material relating to innovations developed during the war.

For many years I have worked with Andrew Mann, of Bae Systems, and he embraced this project with his usual efficiency and enthusiasm. The same applied to the historian, Harry Holmes, the acknowledged expert on the Lancaster Bomber. Andrew was able to provide me with archive material not just relating to aircraft but to Royal Ordnance Factory sites and the Vickers Armstrong complex at Barrow-in-Furness.

My cousin, Alan Hargreaves, was most helpful with regard to the work of wartime civilians at Barrow-in-Furness and through him I met and spoke with Geoff Cain, whose knowledge of Vickers Armstrong evolved as a result of working on the site for around 40 years.

Historical societies have also been valuable sources of material and I was allowed to make use of archives from Bacup Natural History Society, the Pilling Historical Society and the Altcar Territorial Army Camp. To the latter, I was given a guided tour by Commandant Major Bill Hunter.

My thanks are also extended to John Anson, the Features Editor of the *Lancashire Evening Telegraph*, whose continued enthusiasm for this project has been much appreciated.

Without these people, this book would not have been possible and I also owe a debt of gratitude to the staff of Countryside Books. Their encouragement and support enabled me to sail through the stormy waters which assail all those who write books of this type. I hope that those who read this book will feel that the effort has been worthwhile.

Introduction

At first, the idea of finding secret information relating to the Second World War in the old county of Lancashire did not make sense to me. What secrets could the North-West of England have when it was so far distant from the hub of events concentrated in and around London and the South-East? The answer, I discovered, is that it was easier to develop and protect secret inventions in the North-West, which was further removed from the bombing. Furthermore, weapon development required a skilled and hardworking civilian population. Lancashire had these essential ingredients in abundance.

A second question had to be asked as I began to research this book. The German invasion would have come from the Continent, across the Channel and into South-East England. Or would it? Serious consideration was also given in the 1940s to repelling a Nazi invasion via Southern Ireland, landing on the flat, sandy beaches of North-West England and supported by airborne landings.

There was, therefore, a secret war being waged in Lancashire from the late 1930s until peace was declared, and it even continued into the 1950s and 1960s as the 'Cold War' against the Soviet Union began to bite.

This book unravels this secret war waged in the 'old' county of Lancashire. Prior to 1974, Barrow-in-Furness and a substantial area of the Lake District was in Lancashire because the county of Cumbria is a very recent 'invention'. I was born in Barrow-in-Furness in 1936 and my first memories are the sound of bombs falling on the dockland area. September 1940 was a bad time for me. For my fourth birthday I was given a tricycle and, on my first trip, I ran into an old gentleman with a white beard. He was not pleased and I thought that he was Father Christmas! I was convinced that Hitler was coming and, even worse than that, my attack on Father Christmas meant he would not bring me any Christmas presents!

In this book I have tried to unravel some information which the censor kept secret, discover which inventions were developed in Lancashire, and seek out the memories of some of the people who lived and worked here during this traumatic period. If the Germans had landed and gained a foothold in the North-West would there have been 'fighting in the hills'? Indeed there would, and I have succeeded in locating some of these plans, but many people who signed the Official Secrets Act at that time are long dead and their secrets have sadly been buried with them.

I hope that those who read this book and have memories of this period will be inspired to put pen to paper and tell their own stories. There is no reason why events that were secret more than 60 years ago should still be secret today. The history of Lancashire's Secret War should be a proud part of our heritage. If this book helps to lift this veil of secrecy just a little then I will be content.

Ron Freethy

Chapter 1

The Heavy Hand of the Censor

As soon as war was declared in 1939, the heavy hand of the government censor descended upon everyday life all over the country.

In the event of war, it is obviously important that the enemy should be told nothing that might help their cause. It was relatively easy to censor the armed services but it was much more of a problem to persuade civilians that careless talk could indeed cost lives. The people of Lancashire needed even more persuading than most, because initially they felt themselves to be remote from danger, unlike those living in the southern counties. Soon, however, folk began to notice that some of the cotton mills and traditional manufacturing sites were being taken over for the war effort. Rumours began to spread about 'hush-hush' establishments and people began to read the warning posters – 'Be like Dad, keep Mum', 'Walls have ears', 'Tittle tattle lost the battle', plus a host of others – with more than a passing interest.

The evacuation of children away from areas vulnerable to bombing is well known, but many adults associated with secret, or

It was not just children who were evacuated. These girls from the Vickers offices at Barrow were brought by work to Askam-in-Furness. There, sensitive material could be worked on in relative safety.

at least very important, jobs were also moved away from any potential danger. The censor kept a firm grip on the reporting of these movements.

As a young schoolboy at Askam-in-Furness, I lived on what was called the Lots and the school was in the main village. Between the two was a disused ironworks, then called the Furnace but which is now a housing estate. The ironworks' offices were still in a good state of repair as the war started and were occupied by staff who travelled from the Vickers shipyard at Barrow-in-Furness. They dealt with sensitive drawings and other secret papers. At lunchtime the Reverend Chair used to allow some of them to use the vicarage tennis courts and their meals came in by coach from Barrow. The village residents obviously never knew how important this work was and some of the lasses made friends with us young children.

Many civilian movements involved long distances, with workers being placed in permanent billets rather than commuting. Just such a large-scale relocation took place when a Royal Ordnance Factory was purpose-built at Chorley and skilled chemical staff were moved up from Woolwich Arsenal to train the locals. Eventually more than 18,000 people were employed there, but the secret was certainly kept and the vulnerable site was never damaged by bombs or attacked by saboteurs. Emily Bennet, who now lives in Shooters Hill in London, worked there all her life and recalls King George VI and Queen Elizabeth attending the opening of the factory in 1939:

> I remember that it was kept very low key with a civil servant (or should I say censor) in attendance but we were allowed by Mr Burgess to look at the King's signature in the brand new visitors' book. A photograph was taken of the workers and most of us bought one. I was a very lowly pay clerk in those days and I was at the back. As Morecambe and Wise would say, 'I'm the one with the glasses'.

Visits by VIPs anywhere in the country were always kept very

Emily Bennet, the one at the back with glasses, gets a sight of the visitors' book signed by George VI at the opening of the Royal Ordnance Factory at Chorley.

George VI visiting a Metro-Vickers factory at Newton Heath in 1939.

secret and although photographs were taken at the time and published after the visitors had left, even then the precise locations were never released. 'The Prime Minister [or the King and Queen] visited a site in the North-West of England the day before yesterday' was a PR exercise which satisfied the censor.

It is sometimes said that Winston Churchill knew little about Lancashire but nothing could be further from the truth. He was, in the early years of the 20th century, the MP for Oldham and later for Manchester North-West. He spoke regularly throughout Lancashire and, perhaps surprisingly, he was one of the promoters of the Trades Unions Act. He tried to have working hours reduced and those who complained of his slave driving during the war would do well to remember this. He had been the Minister of Munitions in the Lloyd George administration of 1917

The Sumner triplets greeting Prime Minister Winston Churchill.

during the First World War and at that time he was hard on traitors and spies and never failed to point out the need to keep secrets very secret indeed.

Throughout his premiership Churchill was a frequent visitor to Lancashire and on one occasion in 1944 he stopped his car as he saw three little girls who looked to be identical. These triplets, Marjorie, Anne and Elizabeth Sumner, were the first to be born in Blackburn, and I spoke to Anne, who told me that they were shy of the great man but their mother was proud of the meeting and treasured a photograph taken on the day.

The censors did not just concern themselves with high profile establishments and events. It may well have been a case of shutting the stable door after the horse had bolted but all Ordnance Survey maps were immediately removed from sale. After the war it was discovered that the Germans already had all the relevant maps, plus many thousands of copies of the *AA Handbook*.

Further precautions were taken against the enemy to prevent him finding his way around. All milestones and signposts were removed and then put into store for safe-keeping. Most were returned after the war but not always in the exact same place! The names of railway stations were painted out and travellers had to rely on porters with loud voices to ensure that they did not overshoot their destination. The song *Oh Mr Porter what shall I do, I wanted to go to Birmingham and you put me off at Crewe* had more than a ring of truth about it during the war. Train timetables meant nothing in those days and, anyway, were not printed because paper was in short supply, so the censor had no need to act in this respect although old timetables listing the stations in the correct order along the line were pulped.

Civilian casualties were never published during the war and it was only later that it was revealed that 1,005 died in the Manchester blitz and 3,966 were killed in Liverpool. These figures compare with the 1,236 poor souls wiped out in Coventry. Mrs Joyce Kilshaw of Sale, near Manchester, recalls:

> One of my vivid memories of the war was looking each day at the lists which were pinned up informing the neighbourhood who had been killed in the various air raids. However, I am now sure that these lists didn't give quite a full picture of those who lost their lives and most certainly the numbers had been well and truly censored. It was terrible to come out of an air raid shelter in a morning not knowing if you had a house to go home to. Sometimes

A Luftwaffe target photograph taken in 1940 and showing Manchester and Salford docks. Great damage was later done to the area.

news of houses that had been bombed filtered through to
the shelter, but the ARP wardens were told not to give any
information to stop people going out of the shelters whilst
raids were still going on to try to rescue their belongings.
The ARP wardens had to write detailed reports and they
were also censored.

The stray bombs which fell on towns and, sometimes, remote

*Butterfly bombs were aimed mainly at children. Casualties were kept secret so
that the Germans would not be encouraged to drop more.*

villages were reported, but only in the vaguest of terms such as: 'Three people were killed when a bomb struck a Lancashire village.' On 21st June 1940 the *Manchester Guardian* reported that two people were killed by bombs in a 'North-Western town'. This town was Accrington and killed were Mary Robinson aged 65 and her daughter Beatrice. Sixty-six year old Ephraim Robinson died later in hospital.

In schools, posters appeared warning children about picking up unusual looking objects. The commonly accepted view during the war was that these warnings were without substance but this was not true. The most dangerous objects, often brightly-coloured, were attractive-looking weapons which became known as 'butterfly bombs'. They were dropped from aircraft and descended almost helicopter-like. Some landed in trees. Many

German bombs did inflict damage on Trafford Park, as this photograph of the aircraft factory at Metro-Vickers shows. They destroyed the first of the Manchester bombers to be finished and also several others under construction.

Exchange Street Station on 23rd December 1940.

curious youngsters were killed or maimed by them, but the censors hid the true statistics among those killed by conventional bombing. This successfully led the Germans to think that the weapon was an expensive failure and they stopped dropping their deadly butterflies.

A blanket of secrecy was also placed over the V1, or doodlebug, attack on the North-West of England on the morning of Christmas Eve, 1944. According to German records, between 40 and 50 missiles were launched from Heinkel He111 bombers over the Hull area. These passed over the East coast and reached as far as Durham and Shropshire but the Lancashire Pennine area received the brunt of them. Casualties, the numbers all obviously censored, were inflicted at Abbeyhills Road in Oldham, Garners Lane in Stockport, Worsley, and Tottington near Bury. At Tottington, six people were killed and Chapel Street was demolished. This was never rebuilt and a memorial garden now occupies the site.

Victoria Station in Manchester on 24th December.
Both this photograph and the previous one of Exhange Street Station were blocked from publication by the censor.

Other V1s landed on Radcliffe, Hyde and Didsbury, the last mentioned being one of a few which released propaganda leaflets before exploding. These leaflets included quotes from letters said to be written by British prisoners of war and indicating that life in Germany was better than that in Britain under Churchill. They were collected by the police and other authorities and quickly destroyed.

It was not only words which were censored but photographs, showing locations, were also banned. This particularly applied to any showing railway stations and factories. It made good sense but what makes less sense, on first glance, is the censorship of references to disruption by the weather, especially the heavy snowstorms which typified the winters of the 1940s. I spoke about this to Dennis Wood, a retired Manchester policeman, who made the point: 'Heavy snow on the ground obviously did not affect bombers and their targets could have been made easier if trains were stranded in the snow. Hitting a stationary target must have been easier than one moving at high speed. In any case, the censor took the view that it was better to be "safe than sorry".'

The censors worked particularly hard to ensure that the locations of potentially dangerous chemicals were kept secret and the movement of these substances had to be carefully supervised. This also applied to use by specialist hospitals, of which Christies in Manchester was potentially the most vulnerable in Britain.

Christies had been at the forefront of research on radiography from its foundation in the 1890s, when physicians became interested in the growths prevalent among those who worked in the dusty atmosphere of cotton mills. There were also growths on the lips of women who worked in the mills and 'kissed the shuttle', when they threaded the cotton onto the shuttle by using their teeth. In doing this they absorbed lots of potentially damaging substances. Christies became famous for the use of radiography, which meant dealing with really dangerous chemicals. By 1938 the hospital had an established reputation throughout the world, including Germany.

For the duration of the war, it was decided that all hospitals

Snow in Manchester in 1940. Why should we need to keep this a secret from the Germans? Perhaps because they could more easily bomb stationary trains?

using radium must ensure that the material was kept away from the bombing, to ensure that radioactive material could not 'leak' into the environment. It could be used in measured quantities needed by doctors but the bulk of the material had to be kept in holes more than 30 feet deep. Even the construction of a purpose-built pit was not considered adequate and a survey of the mines in Lancashire and Cheshire was undertaken as well as the limestone caverns in the Peak District of Derbyshire.

Eventually Christies decided, with government approval, that the best location was the Blue John Mine at Castleton in Derbyshire, which is a major tourist attraction today just as it was before the war. This 'cave' was an ideal place to keep the radium, where the continual leakage of radon gas could be trapped into glass cells. A piece of glass equipment was specially made to tap off the radon, which had to be done three times each week. The apparatus was so complex to construct that an expert glass-blower was needed and in 1941 a German prisoner of war carried out this task. Obviously he had no clue how important his work was, but he was one of Europe's best glass-blowers.

John Lister, now retired, was at this time a physicist, skilled instrument maker and a vital part of Christies' research programme. It was John's job to visit Castleton to obtain the correct dose for each patient being

John Lister, instrument maker and boffin during World War II at Christies.

treated. Transporting such potentially dangerous material required a police escort.

In 1941 the severe winter weather was a problem when the Castleton electric generator could not operate in the low temperature. It was thus decided that plans must be made to keep the radium safely in the hospital. A piece of equipment had been devised to tap the radon off in the hospital's specially constructed borehole. After protracted negotiations the Government gave Christies permission to bring their stocks back from Castleton.

At this time research into the treatment of cancer proceeded apace and new techniques resulted in what has become known as

An aerial shot of Christie Hospital in 1938. (Manchester Libraries)

Below, the physics laboratory at Christies in the 1940s.

the Manchester Method of treatment. During the war the German threat was ignored, or rather accepted, and the boffins and physicians got on with their essential work! Today, Christies still leads the world in cancer treatment.

Such groundbreaking research costs money and Christies has always been in urgent need of funds; this did not cease during the war. In 1943 the film star Robert Donat appealed for money to be added to the Endowment Fund. The censor, however, looked carefully at the script before it could be broadcast or released to the newspapers.

If it was possible, the grip of the censor became even firmer as preparations for the invasion of France gathered pace. Nowhere was this more obvious than at Ringway Aerodrome, which is now the site of Manchester Airport. Ringway was never officially requisitioned but remained under the control of the Manchester City Council throughout the war. This may, however, have been a cover-up operation.

Ringway performed several military functions and was serviced by a large number of civilians who all had to abide by the Official Secrets Act. Men and women who were already skilled linguists

Apparatus for handling radioactive material.

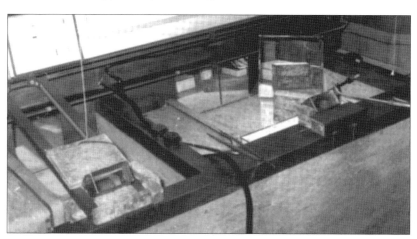

were trained as parachutists here and then dropped into Occupied Europe to liaise with Resistance fighters. Another secret area concerned the project to construct fleets of gliders and train their crews, which operated so successfully during and after the Normandy invasion.

Work also went on to produce a James Bond-type piece of apparatus. This was the Haffner Rotachute, which was a variation of the conventional parachute. It comprised a two-bladed helicopter-like rotor, underneath which was a protected fuselage. This was trialed in the area around Ringway but was not perfected before the end of the war. Like most of the censored material this project remained on the secret list long after the war had finished.

Some of the spy 'stories' during the war were later shown to be true but even to this day precise details have been 'lost'. Dennis Wood, however, did have some success in locating information and told me:

> I managed, at long last, to look at the memoirs of the late Chief Superintendent, Dan Timpany. In 1941 he arrested William Gaskell Downing, a former Air Ministry official, and charged him under the Official Secrets Act with making sketches useful to the enemy. At Manchester assizes Downing was sent to prison for six years. He had made photographic copies of badges and passes which would enable persons to gain access to munitions factories and other establishments from where valuable information, of use to the enemy, could be obtained. These facts came to light when the then Detective Inspector Timpany arrested Downing at an address in Queens Court, Didsbury, Manchester. He was living with a German girl, an illegal immigrant, who was afterwards interned in the Isle of Man. It was stated at Downing's trial, that he had secured a post with the Air Ministry aeronautical inspection department in 1939. He left his wife when he began an association with the German girl the same year. As most enemy agents were executed, or recruited as double agents, his sentence seems

to have been light and it may be that the girl was a spy and merely used Downing, though there is nothing in the file to suggest that.

There are also unconfirmed reports that there were two pleasure steamers operating from Morecambe during the 1930s which were far from innocent. They were called the *Minden* and the *Emden* and they were German-owned. They cruised all along the coast between Morecambe and North Wales, obviously passing close to Liverpool. Gilbert Bradshaw told me that his father, who fought in the First World War, refused to take a pleasure trip on these vessels because he said that 'the Hun were spying'. He was probably right.

Chapter 2

The Secret World of the Jet Engine

There is no doubt that Lancashire played a major role in secret research work in many projects, some of which will be described in the chapters which follow. None had such a high profile, however, as the development of the jet engine.

The concept of jet propulsion had been known for many years but far too few working engineers thought it would work. In 1928 Frank Whittle, then a very junior RAF officer, had published a paper on the use of a gas turbine to power an aircraft. He based this upon theoretical and practical studies which he had conducted; in 1930 he finally patented his engine, under the title of Power Jets. Nobody at the Air Ministry gave him either cash or encouragement and Whittle was obliged to form his own company. His budget was limited.

Meanwhile, Rolls-Royce had also started to develop its own

concept of gas turbine engines. The war was by then foremost in the minds of government ministers, however, and they could not allow Rolls-Royce to spend time on an untried engine – they were forced to devote all their energies to the Merlin project with other piston engines to follow.

Whittle's wonderful discovery therefore faced two problems. Obviously the Germans were also working on jet propulsion, but the Whittle researchers had another 'enemy' and that was those who made decisions on behalf of the British government. The fact that the Rolls-Royce Merlin, which powered first the Spitfire and later the Lancaster, was the best piston engine in the world did not help. This led to the belief in senior circles that the future of aircraft propulsion lay in further improvement of the piston engine.

In retrospect it would seem that the British, under the Whittle team, were ahead in the technological battle whilst the Germans were given more official encouragement to develop both jet and rocket propulsion techniques. What was not in doubt is that both belligerents were intent upon keeping their developments very, very secret.

By the time war broke out even the stubborn (or probably more accurately, short-sighted) Air Ministry politicians had begun to appreciate the potential of the Whittle engine but they were still not prepared to divert resources from Rolls-Royce. Power Jets needed a sponsor and, in January 1940, a meeting took place between Whittle and the Wilkes brothers who owned the Rover Car Company. Then the Air Ministry proved just how devious they could be. In March 1940 they pointed out to Power Jets and Rover that as Whittle was a serving officer, all his patents actually belonged to the government. They would allow Power Jets to develop the new engine but they would determine who would build the production engines.

No wonder Whittle was annoyed and although he worked with the Rover Company, relations with them were strained from the outset. He (Whittle) would do the work whilst Rover built the engines and pocketed the bulk of the profits. The Air Ministry got the rest. Furthermore, Whittle was firmly of the opinion that the

Rover engineers, who were used to producing car engines, were not so competent as others, especially the men from Rolls-Royce, who had already proved their worth in the production of aero-engines.

Neither Stanley Hooker, a prominent Rolls-Royce designer, nor Fred Morley, whom I spoke to on this topic, felt that Rover were treated fairly in this matter but both agreed that Frank Whittle was a delightful man. Fred Morley said to me, 'I'd be bloody narked if I did the work and some other sod made a fortune, especially if I wanted money to improve my engine.'

I have not yet explained why the original Whittle Power Jets-Rover alliance should have been forged first in Clitheroe and then in Barnoldswick. Lord Beaverbrook, heading the new Ministry for Aircraft Production, was quite right in his forceful assertion that there should be 'shadow factories' developed for the production of all vital equipment so that a single bombing raid would not paralyse any one project. It was also important that research work, where there was only one prototype, should be conducted not only in secret but also in relatively safe locations. The designers and workforce also needed to be housed in safety and secrecy.

Thus it was that No 6 shadow factory, which was an old weaving shed, was established at Bankfield in Barnoldswick, initially to build piston engines under licence. Included in this complex scheme were Carleton Mill near Skipton, Grove and Soughbridge Mills at Earby, as well as two other mills in Barnoldswick, which were Calf Hall and Butts Mill. The final link in this chain was Waterloo Mill in Clitheroe. This was the site given to the Whittle team, first to develop and then to negotiate the use of a large factory to get the jet engine into production. The development was obviously carried on in secret but not till Fred Morley's team gave me a photograph of Whittle's first engine did I realize exactly what a spy would have thought if he or she had peeped through the window at night. They would have thought it was a pile of milk churns welded together and tied up with electrical wire!

Not that anyone could have peeped in at night because they would have been spotted by the team who were there beavering away – a 20-hour day would have been the aim for most of them, I

The hamlet of Bracewell is still isolated and during the war it was an ideal base for a team working on a secret project.

suspect. All these shadow factories and the secret research was coordinated from offices based at Bracewell Hall, between Gisburn and Barnoldswick. Few people in the 1940s, or even today, realised what important research was done in this area. Even when they drive through Barnoldswick and see the huge Rolls-Royce factory (which is still developing jet engines to this day), most tend to underrate the importance of the craftsmen (and women) of this area.

Whilst this important work was going on, Frank Whittle continued to feel bitter about his treatment and also had increasing doubts whether Rover could come up with the working engine. By all accounts the Wilkes brothers, who then owned Rover, were not too happy with the arrangement either.

The late Sir Stanley Hooker of Rolls-Royce, in his biography, describes how an acceptable compromise was reached. Ernest Hives, his right-hand man, and Hooker himself knew that there was a future in jet engines and were frustrated that all their spare capacity was taken up by producing Merlin engines and then trying to build ever larger piston engines. If they knew the potential of the jet, then it was reasonable to suppose that the Germans also realised this.

Hives arranged to meet S. P. Wilkes, the Rover boss, for dinner at the Swan and Royal Hotel in Clitheroe. He said to Wilkes, who was expressing alarm at the deteriorating relationship with Whittle, 'I'll tell you what I'll do. I'll give you our tank factory in Nottingham and you give me this jet job in Barnoldswick.' Wilkes replied with alarming speed and one word, 'Done!'

Hooker then went on to explain what happened next in the jet engine saga at Clitheroe and Barnoldswick: 'I was sent there as chief engineer to get this project into production ... within six months the team had the engine tested at its designed thrust of 1,600 pounds. This was the W2B.' By this he meant the Whittle 2B.

The Swan and Royal Hotel in Clitheroe where the historic jet engine deal was agreed.

Hooker was a generous man and he freely acknowledged the initial part played by the best of the Rover engineers.

Many Rover men, including the particularly gifted Adrian Lombard, chose to remain with the Whittle jet and were welcomed into the Rolls-Royce team. The construction of new engines is a complex and painstaking problem but adapting an existing airframe and especially designing a new aircraft to carry the engine is quite another. Both these alternatives were tried.

The Gloster Aircraft Company had the task of developing the Meteor airframe to take the jet engine into the air and this flew on 15th May 1941 at RAF Cranwell. Some idea of the apathy in military circles with regard to the jet is proved by the fact that no official photographer was sent to cover this event!

Trials were also made by fitting twin engines to the rear of two

Britain's first jet fighter, seen here in 1951, was actually successfully flown in 1943. It took time for the authorities to accept that piston engines were a part of history. (BAe Systems)

Barnes Wallis-designed Wellington bombers. At about the same time, the twin engines were fitted into the Meteor, which I remember from my own Air Force days when we called them 'Meat Boxes' because they were so accident prone.

The Rolls-Royce team were soon ready to rename the engine. The Whittle W2B/23 became the Welland, as it was decided to call the future jet engines by the names of rivers to give the impression of the flow which is associated with jet propulsion.

During the course of my work with the BBC I was lucky enough in 1998 to have gathered in one room, courtesy of BAe Systems, four of Whittle's team at that time, all now in their late seventies or eighties and who had helped to devise and build the jet engine. 'We all knew and respected Sir Frank Whittle. We quickly dispelled the oft-quoted myth that Whittle was a difficult man to deal with. I was bloody difficult to deal with when I had a design and it was being buggered up by politicians that didn't know a blueprint from their backside,' grinned the mischievous Fred Morley.

Fred was a project designer and was instrumental in the production of most of the famous jet engines at Rolls-Royce. Then there was Allan Oddie, who is regarded as one of the finest draughtsmen ever to work on jets. Allan was born in Waddington near Blackburn and his skills were honed at Blackburn Technical College. By the age of 16 he was producing detailed working drawings from Morley's sketches: 'There were thousands and thousands of sketches and then detailed drawings for the fitters to work on. We then had a trial engine for Fred Morley to fiddle with.'

'And for us to smash,' chimed in the other two, the mercurial Welshman David Davies and Arthur Redsell, who hailed from Derby and who came to Barnoldswick and remained in the area, living in retirement at Barrowford near Nelson. Arthur loved the Lancashire countryside, jet engines and humour.

'What a job we had – take an engine and run it till it bust. Sounds like a schoolboy's dream doesn't it?'

'Ah,' interrupted Morley, pretending to be fierce, 'but I always wanted to know where it bust and why!'

'An animated milk churn'. The first turbo-jet developed in Lancashire in top secret and, below, the end product – the Rolls-Royce Welland turbo-jet.
(Rolls-Royce Archive)

'I agree,' replied Davies, 'that was the difficult bit.'

Out of this apparent cut and thrust and humour came the best aero-engines in the world, but this is only what you would expect from Rolls-Royce. Royce himself was a perfectionist and as Fred Morley remarked, he expected everybody else to be. 'Actually,' Fred grinned, 'only perfectionists worked for Rolls-Royce – the rest got the sack!'

Some of these engines were more successful than others. The four all liked and respected Stanley Hooker and they also acknowledged the men – and women – who built the engines which they designed. 'It's no bloody good drawing an engine if the damned thing comes apart when you run it. You need good materials and bloody good workmen. Lucas at Burnley were the best in the world for years,' Fred Morley told me and the others agreed. 'They spoke our language – but then that's northern folk for you. They always call a spade a bloody shovel.'

The Birmingham company of Joseph Lucas had been approached by the Ministry of Aircraft Production in 1940 to undertake, in great secrecy, work on a new type of aircraft power unit.

They were to investigate the many combustion problems associated with the production of what became known as the gas turbine. This required new technology, the development and production of stronger alloys and retraining of staff. What was needed was a new factory without making it obvious that something new was afoot. To begin with Lucas built a small factory at Clitheroe close to where the Whittle team were based. Soon it was obvious that this factory was inadequate and a new purpose-built complex was established at Burnley.

Eventually two factories were built at Wood Top and Hargher Clough and from then, until its demise in the 1980s, Lucas produced a regular supply of apprentices recruited from local schools. State-of-the-art research laboratories were also built but during the war nobody knew of their secret work. Skilled male labour, both at Clitheroe and especially at Burnley, was becoming a real problem and the solution was as usual to recruit more women. Mrs Amy Riding recalls:

*The Lucas factories at Burnley employed women to produce ground-breaking
aero-engine developments.*

Me and my two sisters worked at Lucas and as ex-mill lasses the noise of the machines did not worry us. Folk said that learning to weld was dangerous and we had to keep our hair away from everything. So we always wore headscarves. Us folk had worked in a mill and had to keep several looms working at full speed. We were used to keeping our hair away from machines. We did not know until much later what we were making and I thought we were welding parts of exhausts for tanks.

What was actually being produced were the very complex gas turbines used on the Rolls-Royce jet engines which were assembled at Clitheroe and Barnoldswick. Each part had to be machined to a degree of accuracy which, until the impetus of war, would not have been achievable. It was not until 1946 that the plans and diagrams were published and details of the work on the Meteor aircraft and others were released. The complexity of the drawings still amazes me even 60 years after they were drawn. I recall as a schoolmaster in Burnley in the 1960s taking groups of hopeful schoolboys around the Lucas factories and even at that time with the Cold

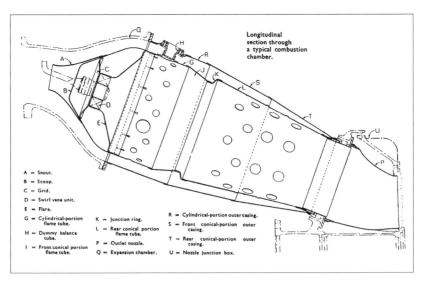

Longitudinal section through a typical combustion chamber.

A = Snout.
B = Scoop.
C = Grid.
D = Swirl vane unit.
E = Flare.
G = Cylindrical-portion flame tube.
H = Dummy balance tube.
I = Front conical portion flame tube.
K = Junction ring.
L = Rear conical portion flame tube.
P = Outlet nozzle.
Q = Expansion chamber.
R = Cylindrical-portion outer casing.
S = Front conical-portion outer casing.
T = Rear conical-portion outer casing.
U = Nozzle junction box.

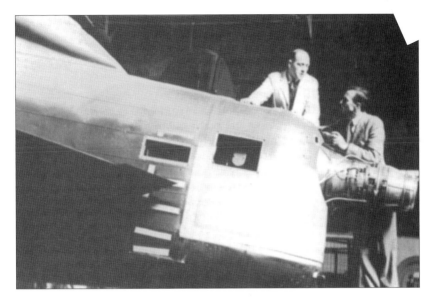

In 1944 other companies were adapting aircraft for jet engines. Here it is fitted to a Lancaster.

War still at arctic levels there were research areas which were not open to the public.

It was in the 1940s, however, that the men and women working in the Burnley factories played such an important part in keeping Britain ahead of Germany in the secret technological war. One of the boffins at Lucas during the war was the handsome 'Pop' Ifield who, despite his name, was a young Australian and an expert on high performance fuel pumps. Neil Barnes recalled:

> I had two hobbies which were aero engines and pop music. 'Pop' had the same interestes and his son Frank Ifield later became one of the world's pop stars of the 1960s and 1970s.

The Germans were no fools and there is no reason to think that they did not have spies in the area. Bombs dropped 'by accident' at

Burnley and Clitheroe, were said to have been dumped by German planes to lighten their load. Perhaps they did in fact attempt to hit the factories and the bombs which fell in these areas may actually have been aimed. Alas, we will never know but the presence of such important and secret locations would suggest vulnerable targets, which local people would not have been aware of.

The village of Chatburn, for instance, which is between Clitheroe and Barnoldswick, had a mill which could possibly have been a 'shadow' factory researching the jet – in the opinion of the German High Command. Actually, the mill was producing the pull-through fabric for cleaning rifles. On Wednesday, 30th October 1940, the village was bombed and the newspapers reported that: 'Bombs fell on a North-West village which killed two [later three] people and injured several others.'

Two bombs fell on Chatburn during that daylight raid and eyewitnesses reported that the pilot circled the mill twice before dropping the bombs. This to me looks like a planned raid on the mills. This makes more sense than the old theory that the bombs were dumped to lighten the load. Why circle twice and appear to aim if the object was only to lighten the aircraft? One large bomb also fell on Thompson's Park at Burnley, which was actually quite close to the Lucas factories.

One aspect of the war in the air, which is hardly mentioned at all, concerns the fuel needed to run the engines. All the oil entering

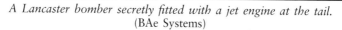

A Lancaster bomber secretly fitted with a jet engine at the tail.
(BAe Systems)

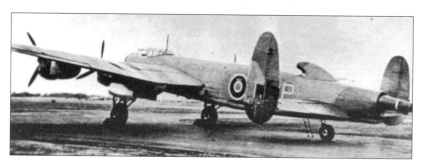

The Canberra team: (left to right) Don Crowe, Dai Ellis, Harry Harrison, Alf Elison, Teddy Petter, Roly Beaumont (test pilot), Denis Smith, Freddy Page and Hugh Howat.

Britain had to be brought in by sea and these supply lines were an obvious target for U-boats and marauding German aircraft, as were areas where the crude oil was processed. If the supply of aviation fuel failed then the war would be lost.

Dirty and poorly processed fuel would have caused engine problems both for piston and jet engines. An improved high-octane aviation fuel had to be developed in great secret and, obviously, in an isolated place. Gilbert Bradshaw recalls:

> The site chosen was close to what became after the war the Middleton Towers Holiday Camp between Heysham and Overton. The reason for this choice was that the site was close to a harbour and with good road and rail links. Development began in 1938 as a joint enterprise between the Trinidad Oil Company, Shell and ICI. The Trinidad Oil Company soon backed out to leave Shell and ICI to perfect a high-octane aviation fuel to improve the performance, in the first instance, of Hurricanes and Spitfires with the pilots trying to get every tiny advantage over their German

Canberras under construction at Samlesbury.

opponents. The fuel was called Trimpel and the research
unit continued to operate until the 1950s.

From the projects described in this chapter alone it can be seen
that Lancashire played an important and perhaps major role in the
secret development of aviation during World War Two. What
should be mentioned, however, is that at the end of the war not all
the secret establishments were shut down. Nowhere is this better
illustrated than in the case of the Canberra fighter-bomber. This
wonderful aeroplane kept thousands of Lancashire civilians in
work for 50 years!

Initially, the project did not begin in Lancashire and it was not
called the Canberra. It all began at the Westland Works at Yeovil
in Somerset. This factory then decided that it wanted to

Mock up of the Canberra cockpit.

concentrate on the production of helicopters. In 1943, under a cloak of secrecy, Westland designer Teddy Petter had begun work on a high altitude and very fast light bomber, but Project E3/45 was not considered to be important. Then came one of the most significant 'free transfers' in the history of aviation. Teddy Petter and his equally able assistant, Glen Hubday, were allowed to move to the English Electric Works on Strand Road in Preston.

The team which produced the aircraft soon known as the Canberra proved to be a world-beater. A great deal of very secret work went on and it was only in late 1946 that any details at all leaked out. The project was then described as the development of a 'high altitude bomber'. It could cruise at 500 miles per hour and fly at up to 45,000 feet carrying a bomb load of 6,000 pounds. Furthermore, it had a range of 1,600 miles!

The work at Preston was helped by the availability of the jet engines being perfected in Lancashire at the Rolls-Royce factories in the Clitheroe and Barnoldswick area. It was also important to recruit skilled workers who knew how to keep a secret, as Philip Turner recalls:

> I was ambitious and wanted to be accepted as aircrew. The RAF communications flight based at Samlesbury had an old Oxford aircraft; I was once allowed to fly it under dual control. In June 1944, much to my chagrin, I was moved to a very hush-hush department set up in a former garage in Corporation Street, Preston. The nucleus of a design staff was being set up there to put into design and eventual production what became known as the Canberra. I saw the prototype literally take shape on the drawing board. There were two or three trial paper versions; one had a single engine in the belly and another was a single-engined version with twin booms. All these were obviously kept very secret but the final version was a twin-engined aircraft very like the wooden model which Mr. Petter brought with him from Westlands.

Wing spurs of a Canberra. The holes to the right are the holes for the jet pipes.

In 1999, whilst producing a series of BBC radio programmes, I was shown the diagrams, models and photographs relating to the Canberra. A sure indication of the success of the design was that Canberras were still operational nearly 50 years on.

Chapter 3

The Battle of the Boffins

The 1930s saw bumper audiences in the cinema and young and old were brought up on a diet of Flash Gordon, the Evil Emperor Ming, the death ray and lethal gases. Many expected our own boffins not only to understand the science fiction but also to improve upon it!

Meanwhile, veiled in a cloak of secrecy, university and military experts were intent upon keeping up with or even ahead of not only the Americans (which did not matter in military terms) but also the highly efficient German scientists, who were certain to be much more of a problem. In the 1930s Winston Churchill, thankfully as things turned out, fanned the flames of concern and when he became Prime Minister he was keen to promote all scientific innovations.

Nowhere was the battle for scientific supremacy more focused than upon the development of radar. The subject fascinated researchers at universities all over the country including those in the North-West of England.

The development of a radar system obviously had to be 'boffin based'. This research was not the remit of a clutch of mad professors or a writer of science fiction. Serious scientists had to take the front seat and their experiments had to be conducted in great secrecy. Robert Watson-Watt was the bright young hope at the National Physical Laboratory based at Slough, but he was in close touch with scientists and mathematicians at Manchester University. They had all read a report published by the Post Office which said that aircraft flying through their radio beams were interrupting their radio signals. It was realised that this discovery could be adapted to detect aircraft and here we have the basic concept for the development of RADAR – RAdio Detection And Ranging.

By January 1937 Watson-Watt knew enough to persuade the authorities to provide him with a budget of £10 million to develop radar and a chain of linked stations, initially covering the South-East coast but later and in great secrecy spreading to other areas including the North-West of England. At first a device operated from the top of Blackpool Tower but later a major unit was established at nearby Inskip. This is still a vital communications unit today.

The system of early warning in operation at the start of the war depended solely on the members of the Royal Observer Corps and the ability of these men and women to distinguish between enemy and friendly aircraft often at very high altitudes was obviously vital. By 1940 an efficient network was operating in the South-East and by 1941 the whole of the country was linked via a network of well-trained observers. These were grouped into Alarm Officers and Alarm Controllers and involved a combination of visual observations and increasingly sophisticated radar and radio communications. Observation posts were set up in secret locations all over the country: windmills on the Fylde were used, as were Blackpool Tower, as mentioned above, and Lancaster Castle.

Around 1,500 members of the Royal Observer Corps were co-opted into the Merchant Navy on the DEMS project – Defensively Equipped Merchant Ships. Many were from Lancashire and served

A mock-up of an Observer post early in 1940.

on the Atlantic Convoys. They became known as 'Seaborne Observers' and they also played a vital role in the Normandy Invasion. On land, the Ministry of Home Security installed Air Raid Warning Offices at centres some distance from the Royal Ordnance factories to provide an early warning of aircraft approaching these weapons establishments. The Royal Observer Corps has as its badge a beacon light typical of Elizabethan times, the Tudor variant of an early warning system.

The 50,000 men and women observers were very efficient in daylight – almost certainly more efficient than the early radar. Visual observations, however, were obviously of much less use at night and this was where radar would prove so invaluable.

Work with radio beams of a slightly different nature was being carried out in the 1930s at the Ferranti works near Manchester. They had a Gypsy Moth aircraft (G-AAKN) based at Blackley Golf

---

A newspaper cutting helping to identify German aircraft.

Course and used by Sir Vincent de Ferranti in his experimental work. This involved using a narrow radio beam as an assistance to navigation. The beam could be directed at a target and all the aircraft navigator had to do was to fly along this beam. The company knew that the Germans were also conducting similar experiments and Ferranti kept their own scheme under wraps. Once the war became inevitable the company had to work out how to disrupt this beam. Later it was postulated that the Ferranti device actually 'bent' the beam and thus pushed the bomber off track but this is not quite correct. What they produced was a jamming device which rendered the navigational beam or beams useless.

The very sophisticated German method was to follow two radio beams which intersected over the target. The project, which was called Knickebein, was discovered by Allied agents. Radio Counter Measures (RCMs) were developed and units were soon operating all over the UK which disrupted one or both of these beams, in some cases directing the enemy aircraft to fake 'Starfish' locations (see chapter 6).

Such precise equipment as that involved in the development of radar and navigational beams needed to have an able mathematician to work out the complex calculations as quickly as possible. It is at this point that Lancashire-based scientists led the world. What became known as the Hartree Differential Analyser was in fact the world's very first efficient computer.

Douglas Rayner Hartree was born into a family of Cambridge scientists and became Professor of Mathematics at Manchester University. He built his first Analyser from Meccano parts and then had it scaled up and precision-made by Metro-Vickers in Manchester's Trafford Park. The Analyser proved to be a versatile machine but as with modern computers, it was only as good as the data which was fed into it. There were occasions when government officials over-estimated the power of the machine and under-estimated Hartree's own abilities and those of his students.

When the first German magnetic mine was recovered (see chapter 8) there were questions which had to be answered relating to its

Hartree's first Differential Analyser (above), built in 1935 from Meccano, and (below) the scaled up machine in use. Hartree is standing on the left in the top photograph and on the right below. Compare the Analyser's size with a modern hand-held computer.

fusing and firing. A team from the Admiralty travelled all the way to Manchester to ask Hartree to operate his machine to calculate their requirements. The man himself sat down at his desk and gave them all the answers in less than two hours without operating the machine at all. At this time the Analyser was considered to be so secret that it was located in a cellar deep in the bowels of the physics laboratories of Manchester University.

The machine was used to calculate the solutions to many vital developments, including a device to develop the steering of tanks by radar towards a target which the driver could not see, through any of the obstacles in the way. Anti-aircraft guns could likewise be locked onto a target at night. The automatic control of chemical factories was also worked out using the Analyser.

The Analyser also proved to be invaluable in the prediction of the eccentric motion of an aircraft following engine or rudder failure. This allowed instruments to be developed which the pilot could use to counteract these problems and give the crew time to escape by parachute or even for the plane to get safely back to base.

A meeting at Great Westminster House, on 20th March 1942, resulted in the setting up of a panel, with members consisting of the Admiralty, Ministry of Supply, Ministry of Aircraft Production, Hartree's team and ten firms including Ferranti and Metropolitan-Vickers. This panel met monthly and both the agenda and the minutes were kept secret. What became known as the 'Differential Analyser Job Shop' was crucial to the functioning of this panel. Among the topics examined were the calculations relating to rocket propulsion and how to track and destroy these missiles, which were far superior to anything available to the Allies. Other topics of interest to the team were radio and also weather forecasting. In his youth, Hartree was an expert on the subject of how atmospheric conditions, especially at high altitude, affected radio signals. He was also interested in radio telescopes and one of his students was Bernard Lovell, who later devised the Jodrell Bank apparatus, which is still a world leader to this day.

Radar, underwater explosives and atomic bomb research all required the use of the Differential Analyser and the politicians made the decision that all sensitive information should be passed on to the Americans who 'might' in turn be prepared to share their researches. Some in the Job Shop queried the word 'might' and were reluctant to share their discoveries until they themselves had written them up in a scientific journal. Clearly in war conditions this was not possible and the politicians' decree was carried out. Many Americans did not, however, see fit to share their findings.

The Manchester machine reached its peak during the war years but later the large, mechanically-operated calculator was replaced by smaller and faster electronic machines. At first these were powered by as many as 2,000 large valves but the modern home computer is many times more powerful than Hartree's Differential Analyser. Efficiency, however, is still due to the intelligence of the programmer.

If Manchester had a wonderful machine of use during the war, then so did its rival city of Liverpool. From 1763 the Port of Liverpool had a signal station sited on Bidston Hill on the Wirral bank of the Mersey estuary. From this flags could be used to pass semaphore messages to warn city merchants that their sailing vessels were approaching their berths. The area of Liverpool called Exchange Flags was once the viewing point where telescopes could be focused on the signallers on Bidston Hill. In 1866 the Bidston Observatory was built but, as early as the 1840s, a one o'clock cannon was fired to enable the skippers of vessels to check their chronometers. This was only interrupted during the two world wars.

In the 1920s, work went on to produce what became known as the world's best tidal predicting machine. This huge machine used all the technological data incorporating the effect of the moon and other minor planetary information on tides and by the time of the Second World War the Bidston machine had become a vital factor in planning seaboard landings. It was dismantled and re-assembled in an underground bunker with its staff sworn to secrecy and given round the clock protection – or should the correct term be surveillance?

All marine operations involved very accurate tidal predictions and this was a major factor in the orders relating to the Atlantic Convoys. These were organised from yet another underground bunker, this time beneath the Pier Head at Liverpool. Here the Battle of the Atlantic was planned and the site is now a fascinating museum. There was a direct electronic link between the Pier Head Operations Room and Bidston.

The Tide Prediction Machine was vital during the build-up to the Normandy invasion and also during the American landings on the Pacific Islands occupied by the Japanese. The machine was well capable of providing accurate information regarding tide times and levels anywhere in the world.

At the end of the war the machine was returned to a more prominent position and during the 1980s, whilst working for Granada Television, I was allowed to watch the machine working.

The Tide Prediction Machine, constructed at Bidston.

*One of the dials of the
Tide Prediction Machine.*

There were cogs, wheels, pulleys, clocks and other assorted machinery, which were only replaced by computerised equipment in the 1990s. The new equipment is obviously much smaller but is actually no more accurate. The old machine has now been dismantled and is due to be re-assembled and displayed by a team from the Liverpool Museum.

The solution to another wartime problem was produced in Lancashire. The First World War had taken its toll on Britain's timber supplies and in 1919 the Forestry Commission was set up with the object of planting trees as quickly as possible. Fast growing non-native conifers were the obvious solution, despite their ugly appearance especially when planted in regimented rows. Even these trees, however, were not ready for harvesting by the time the Second World War began.

Between the wars, research work had been carried out into the use of pre-stressed concrete, initially developed to be a substitute for timber. Limestone was readily available in parts of Britain, including Clitheroe, and quarries were kept hard at work crushing the stone to produce concrete. As research continued, concrete was proved to be even stronger than timber and was used to produce railway sleepers and as a substitute for timber roof beams. This type of concrete does not crack under the twisting pressure when subject to heavy loading. Reinforced concrete found many uses

Factories like this one near Clitheroe were hard at work during the war producing concrete from the limestone quarries.

during the war for air raid shelters, pillboxes, huts for military camps, aircraft hangars and runways. Before the war, airfields were just that – fields, which soon became bogs following rain or snow melt.

Experiments also showed that given the right design and physical calculations, structures made of pre-stressed concrete could be made to float. Tons of the material were used in the construction of the Mulberry harbours during the Normandy invasion of June 1944, forming breakwaters on the French coast which could provide a safe harbour for the invading forces. The various sections of the Mulberry harbours were built in great secrecy and code-named Operation Phoenix. Lytham, on the Ribble estuary, was one area of construction as John Mullen recalls: 'We thought we were building gun emplacements and nobody knew until long after the war what we were making. It is still regarded as a secret

Peter Ainsworth, aged 86, next to a piece of Mulberry harbour on Gold Beach, Arramanches, Normandy.

because once you have learned to keep your mouth shut you never know who you tell. I suppose it's OK to tell you.'

I don't think he will be prosecuted and neither will I when we consider that the Mulberries now lie almost in ruins, but still remembered with affection by the Norman French. The Mulberry project cost some £40 million and the harbours were constructed rather like a gigantic jigsaw. The logistics of transporting these across the Channel and assembling them was nothing short of miraculous.

Lancashire not only played a part in Operation Phoenix but was also involved in the Pipeline Under the Ocean project, which was code-named Pluto. This was no Mickey Mouse operation but an enormous enterprise designed to supply the invading Allies with fuel, via the Isle of Wight and then under the sea to the Normandy Beachhead. To have all the oil tankers needed berthed at the Isle of Wight or even at Portsmouth or Southampton would have been unwise. Lord Beaverbrook insisted that 'all eggs should not be placed in one basket' and devised the concept that each vulnerable resource had to be spread around. The Pluto pipeline therefore involved both Manchester and Liverpool docks.

At the Manchester docks was a gantry several hundred yards long and built to allow the direct loading of the Pluto pipeline, eventually leading to the Isle of Wight area from where the supply was coordinated. It is difficult even these days to imagine the hard labour which must have been needed to dig and protect a trench over this vast distance.

Bob Harvey who still lives in Liverpool, told me of his part in Pluto: 'This obviously involved a lot of back breaking digging but none of us had a clue what we were involved in. It just seemed strange that we were not being called up. Some of the girls called us shirkers and even worse. It was only much later that it leaked out what we had been doing.'

American and British tankers lined up to discharge their oil at a point close to the site later occupied by the Liverpool Garden Festival of 1984. The start of the unloading area is still marked by a yellow buoy. Pluto worked to perfection and lots of Liverpool lads like Bob Harvey laboured long and hard in a construction of which they knew nothing.

Another little known aspect of Lancashire at War is that oil was secretly produced, processed and fed into the Pluto system in the area around Formby between Liverpool and Southport.

'Moist and mossie turffes are digged up which serve the inhabitants for fewell and light', noted Camden here in 1637, describing peat impregnated with what was obviously oil. This free supply of 'black gold' continued until the early 1930s. In 1934 the Government nationalised oil exploration in Britain but appointed consultancy firms to look for fuel. At Formby, the D'Arcy Exploration Company began to drill in earnest and were eventually successful.

As war became inevitable a cloak of secrecy enveloped the Formby Field. More than 50 wells were sunk and the product was processed and connected directly into the Pluto link. It has been estimated that these wells produced around three million gallons of

An old steam locomotive on the site at Lytham Creek where parts of the Mulberry harbour were constructed in large sheds and in great secrecy.

The Mulberry harbours were constructed in the manner of a massive jigsaw.

oil, but they were abandoned in 1966 as other areas of the world could produce the fuel more cheaply.

The production of glass is one of those vital industries which has received scant attention when the war effort is discussed. Yet where would we have been without optical instruments, searchlights, windscreens, cockpits, portholes and periscopes, or in the development of night vision and numerous other products without research into glass? Here Lancashire played a vital role as Pilkington's glassworks in St Helens was Britain's largest producer.

The reputation of German optical instruments was well known, but once the supply of these ran out British glassmakers had to rise to these standards and produce equally high quality instruments. Pilkington's workforce met this challenge. During the war the scientists at Pilkington's were also employed in producing the toughest possible glass for particular use in bullet-proof vehicles and aircraft windows and cockpits, with aircraft flying ever faster

The use of gas masks in the First World War – the legacy of pictures like these was in everyone's minds as the Second World War loomed.

and higher and therefore subject to high pressure. The history of glass is graphically portrayed in the Pilkington Glass Museum.

One fear which thankfully was never realised was that the enemy would attack using poisonous gas. This was no new worry. On 3rd March 1916, Sgt Benjamin Birchenough, a soldier from Burnley, had described the precautions taken on the Western Front:

> Since I came out here I have been through a class of instruction in the use of the gas helmet and for defence in gas attacks. We were put right through the whole business even so far as being closed up in a dug out and having the full force of gas turned on. It was surprising the effect the gas had on our clothing, especially the buttons which were turned green and black but the helmets are splendid.

He was killed at Ypres less than one month later. His words, however, portray the fear of gas attacks, which were expected throughout the Second World War. In the event gas was not used

Between 1939 and 1945 regular 'gas exercises' were carried out by Civil Defence workers. This scene in Manchester in 1940 shows how seriously the threat was taken.

but this was probably because both sides knew that each had ample supplies.

Prior to the war some 3.8 million gas masks were in store and decontamination centres were set up in hundreds of locations; often local churches and their associated institutes were set aside for this. In Bury, Limefield Methodist church was one as was the Brunswick Methodist sports hall. Some works and especially transport departments had their own decontamination plans and this was certainly the case in Manchester and Liverpool. Regular simulated gas attacks were organised and supplies of soap were provided as a smear of this was said to prevent the visors of the masks from misting over. Tons of bleach were kept in secret locations as this was considered to be the best decontaminating agent. Bury had lists of bleach supplies in store and prior to 1939

Manchester Corporation's decontamination squad ready for a gas attack.

*Below: Modern view of the ICI factory at Thornton, now closed.
It was a very secret establishment during the war.*

The laundry was a vital part of factories producing chemicals and filling munitions. This team operated at the ICI works at Thornton.

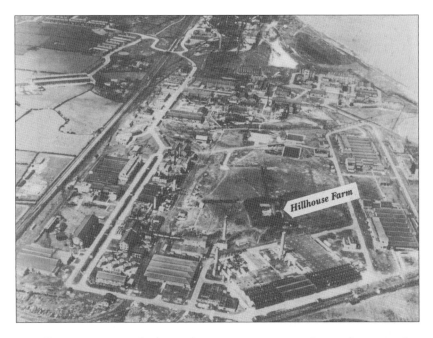

Hillhouse Farm was the base of 'secret' constructions during the war and built by the Ministry of Supply.

had 60,000 gas masks stored in a yard at Fernhill. Masks were also designed for babies and some enterprising people produced masks for their pets and made good profits before supplies of raw materials became limited.

The ARP (Air Raid Precautions) was active in every town and in Bury more than 300 gas detection centres were initiated. These were simply painted boards, which changed colour when they came in contact with gas. Bury also appointed Mr A.C. Dodman as the Gas Identification Officer; he was an ideal appointment because he was the chemistry master at Bury Grammar School!

Throughout the conflict work was going on to produce chemical weapons even though they were not used. At the ICI plant at Thornton on the banks of the River Wyre near Fleetwood, a secret laboratory was at work in addition to the normal chlorine-based manufacturing processes. Chlorine is a green gas which had long been known as a chemical which kills bacteria even when greatly diluted in water. This is why it is used in swimming baths and in water supplies. In high concentrations it is lethal to all life forms and was one of the main components in the gas used during the First World War.

For almost a century the brine wells on the opposite side of the river had been a valuable resource. A pipeline ran under the Wyre from Preesall to serve the ICI factory, which was producing detergents. At the start of the war the Ministry of Works took over the site and built a second pipeline (a sort of mini-Pluto), which served a new factory on the site of Hillhouse Farm. Under great secrecy chlorine and its phosgene derivative-based chemicals were produced. This was obviously a 'poison gas factory', no doubt one of many spread throughout Britain wherever brine could be obtained locally. Thankfully these stocks never had to be used, but what would have happened if the Germans had succeeded in their invasion plans we can only wonder.

Chapter 4

The World's Largest Munitions Filling Factory

As war became inevitable, three things were realised by the Government. Firstly, the Germans were aware of existing armament factories in Britain. Secondly, urban expansion meant that, in times of peace, some once isolated ordnance areas had become incorporated into the heart of expanding cities – of which Woolwich Arsenal was the best example. Thirdly, the volume of explosives needed was likely to be much greater even than that demanded during the First World War; an intensive aerial bombing war was a certainty. New and huge ordnance works had to be quickly purpose-built and Lancashire, being more remote from the Luftwaffe's European bases, was a prime target for government planners.

Emily Bennet, who worked for the Royal Ordnance for more than 40 years, recalls the beginning of the factory near Chorley:

I remember my great aunt Jane who lived in Pear Tree Lane, Euxton telling me that they had erected a hut on the daffodil field. Thus the rumours were confirmed to my family that there was to be a munitions factory on this picturesque countryside, and an area of perimeter fencing was put up which measured around seven miles. My great aunt used to tell me of carrying water from the spring near Buckshaw Hall, which was also a popular country walk for the folk of Chorley. The hall remains today even though the Royal Ordnance Factory (ROF) has gone and it has given its name to Buckshaw Village which is now a housing development.

From this single hut the world's largest munitions filling factory was developed and spread over 928 acres (371 hectares); it involved the compulsory purchase of seven farms. But why this site as opposed to an equally remote area in another and equally safe region elsewhere in the country? A combination of factors meant that Chorley was an ideal choice. These included good access, especially to the railway system with linking lines on a level gradient, which reduced construction to a minimum, whilst the presence of surrounding hills meant that navigation for German bombers would be difficult. The local soil was also carefully analysed and it proved to be sandy, which helped drainage and so not only reduced costs but also made excavation somewhat quicker. Perhaps a crucial factor was that there was a good supply of local labour. Even so, the construction of a factory where some 18,000 people eventually worked did mean that many people had to be brought in and also accommodated.

During the late 1930s three basic types of munitions factories were planned and these were deliberately kept separated. There was a network of factories producing guns, mountings and shell casings; some of these were purpose-built but there were lots of iron foundries in Lancashire and elsewhere which could do the job, whilst cotton mills proved to be ideal spaces in which to produce shell cases. There were also factories producing explosives and these were sited in areas away from high-density civilian housing but close enough to be linked by rail. Thirdly, there were factories which had the cases and the chemicals delivered to them to be filled and primed. Thus the import of raw materials and the export of finished weapons required even greater security and this was why Chorley's new site was constructed specifically for the purpose.

Secrecy was therefore vital and this in itself caused building problems – some sensitive elements were left off the plans and the constructors had to work by 'word of mouth' provided on the spot by those in the know. This obviously played havoc with estimates but despite going over budget the factory was built on time and in a very efficient manner. The civilian contractor selected was Sir Lindsay Parkinson who hailed from Blackpool and could speak the same language as the workmen (and later women) he employed. The building work initially involved some 4,000 civilian tradesmen and labourers plus a huge demand for timber, bricks, cement and steel. Such was the element of danger that each building had to be fitted with a sophisticated system of lightning conductors. A huge and reliable water supply had to be provided and this was extracted from the pipeline linking Thirlmere and Haweswater in the Lake District with Manchester. The pipe itself was vulnerable to attack and this was a worry, as the new factory needed at least two million gallons of good quality water each day.

Despite the snow-bedevilled winters typical of this period construction went on at an accelerating pace and the first shell was filled at 3 pm on 4th December 1938. This was kept a secret from the outside world. Not only was good news censored, though, but care was also taken to avoid bad news spreading. There was an uproar from local people when it was realised that the staff brought north from Woolwich Arsenal were paid more than the locals. The London rate for a 47-hour week was £4 14s 7d whilst the Lancashire equivalent rate was £2 19s 8d.

Another well-kept secret involved the health risks associated with handling explosives especially, as it later transpired, the dangers of exposure to TNT (tri-nitro-toluene). Until late in the war all

*Many cotton mills like this one in Burnley were adapted for munitions work.
Here are shell cases awaiting onward delivery to safe country areas for
filling with explosives.*

Preparing the site for the new Royal Ordnance Factory at Chorley.

explosives were poured into the weapons by hand using small kettles. Anaemia, toxic jaundice and gastritis were the main problems but those in contact with the composition explosive (CE) found that their skin became yellow and so did their overalls and underclothes. Dermatitis was also a problem but despite this some workers seemed reluctant to use either gloves when working or to wash with a 'chemical soap' when they finished a shift.

In an explosives factory the discipline had to be strict and workers were searched to ensure that they did not carry matches, lighters or metal objects which could cause a spark when working in the danger areas. For obvious reasons the buildings were kept far apart and this meant that workers had also to become walkers. Each building was covered with thick layers of earth for camouflage.

Every employee was vetted and those with far right or far left sympathies were weeded out. Many workers in sensitive areas had

*Civilian workers were employed by Sir Lindsay Parkinson
of Blackpool to construct the Royal Ordnance Factory
at Chorley.*

to sign the Official Secrets Act and their credentials were checked at regular intervals.

Safety training was of paramount importance and from figures released after the war it would seem that the measures were successful. In 1942, for example, there were 1,700 'incidents' but by 1944 this figure was reduced to 260 and in 1945 there were only 70 reported 'incidents'. Workers were eventually provided with more suitable protective headgear, overalls and overshoes and there were regular checks for what was called 'static'. The real test, however, is that throughout the war not one major explosion occurred at Chorley.

Just how vast the site was could only be appreciated by those who worked there and had to travel around. One such was Emily Bennet, who worked in the Pay Office:

> On the pay run, as we called it, we could see how huge the site was. We were picked up as early as five in the morning in a big van in order to deliver money to the night shift. We went to both the 'clean' and 'dirty' areas. This meant that operatives changed their clothing in the dirty area before putting on newly laundered clothing in order to work in the clean area where the explosives were placed in the weapons. Before moving into this area each worker was frisked just to make sure that they could not produce sparks of any kind. The laundry on site was huge and so was the tailor's shop, which produced clothing for the operatives. Then there were textile stores plus other stores and huge canteens, which were used by nearly 20,000 people. We were like a town and we even had our own leisure and sports facilities. At the end of the war there were about 1,500 buildings.

Emily Bennet's feeling for the size of the site was echoed by Peter Ainsworth when I spoke to him at his home in Chorley:

> I was employed as a youth on the construction of the factory. I was on the maintenance side, first checking up on

Workers at ROF Chorley filling one of the 'Big Bombs' ready for delivery to the RAF.

the progress of the buildings and later recording faults which were reported as people moved in. There were two hostels, each of which held 2,000 people and which later became educational establishments including teacher training. At Woodlands there was another hostel, this one holding 1,000 people each having their own small room. Many women came from the Newcastle area to work at the factory and they certainly gave lads like me the run around as we asked them what faults they found in their rooms. 'There are no fellas in 'em,' was a regular taunt.

Initially Chorley's function was to provide munitions for the Army because the Navy had provided for itself for centuries. After Dunkirk in 1940 the British Army was able to build up its stocks whilst the Germans were busily engaged in other areas of Europe. For some reason German factories worked a 'normal day' at this time whilst Britain was on a shift system and could work for 24 hours, thus increasing production.

One very secret operation performed at Chorley was the filling of huge bombs. Chorley also filled incendiaries and medium bombs but its role in the Big Bomb Saga only emerged long after the war. In 1943 the factory filled the bouncing bombs designed by Barnes Wallis to destroy the dams along the Ruhr Valley. Strictly speaking the 'bouncing bombs', dropped by Lancashire-built Lancasters, were not circular but barrel-shaped and detonated by the increasing pressure when dropped in water. They should therefore be classed as a mine. Later 12,000-pound Tallboy bombs, which proved so effective towards the end of the war, were also filled at Chorley.

Once it is realised that the weapons had to be loaded in liquid form by hand it is easy to understand how labour-intensive the factory was. The filling involved the use of a device known as a kettle, which was just that. Actually there were two basic methods. In the first, TNT was melted and mixed with a carefully measured quantity of ammonium nitrate. This produced a paste called amatol and a machine known as a worm, which worked like an icing bag on a cake, was used to load it. This was highly dangerous unless care was taken and each operative worked in a thick-walled steel cubicle.

The second method of filling involved melting the amatol paste in steam-heated kettles. The potentially lethal fluid was poured into the shells which were progressed on a rubber-lined conveyor belt. The explosive was then left to solidify and the bombs were later checked to ensure that all sections were in working order.

Another secret was the location of the explosives stores. The various materials were colour-coded and the workers here were checked very carefully for colour-blindness. Kept at Chorley were large stocks of picric acid, ammonium nitrate, gunpowder, magnesium, aluminium, amatol, torpex, fumyl, fulminate TNT and CE. This was a secret cocktail mixed according to the needs of the various armed services. It was obviously vital that these materials were distributed over a wide area and not all stored in one place. Only a very few key workers on site knew the locations

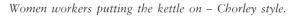

Women workers putting the kettle on – Chorley style.

of all the explosive stores and this information was marked 'most secret'.

Apart from explosives for large weapons, Chorley also produced many thousands of time fuses, which were a vital component of sabotage operations carried out in various overseas locations. In the event of a successful German invasion large numbers of these time fuses would have 'disappeared' and many had already been secretly distributed. A few key individuals had also been trained to 'neutralise' the factory itself.

The workers did keep 'mum' but they all felt under pressure, not only from working long hours but also concerning the material they were dealing with and the feeling that sooner or later they would be targeted by the enemy. They needed to let off steam occasionally. Emily Bennet recalled:

> Of course we were all aware of the dangers but all of us just wanted to get the war won. Even in an atmosphere as strained as this we had our fun. There were facilities for us to enjoy sport and I played hockey and tennis. There were competitions between the various sections and occasional matches against other RO factories at places such as Risley, Lower Darwen, Kirkby near Liverpool and Ellesmere Port. The Americans had a Red Cross House in St Thomas's Road in Chorley where their military men could enjoy coffee and doughnuts. No alcohol was served but some of the ROF girls did not need these stimulants and dated Americans and some became GI brides.

Miss Celia Babskey of Manchester worked for the ROF at Ellesmere Port along with a group of other girls. In their spare time they mixed with injured British servicemen: 'We were pleased that we were making the munitions to enable these lads to fight back once their injuries were dealt with and they were fit again.'

Entertainment was also provided on site and in 1938 Gracie Fields came to Chorley ROF to sing in the Opening Gala. The song *The Biggest Aspidistra in the World* apparently 'went down a

Girls from the Royal Ordnance Factory at Ellesmere Road entertaining wounded soldiers, September 1944. (Celia Babskey)

bomb', though perhaps this is not quite the right phrase to use in this context!

The last word on the Royal Ordnance Factories in the North-West of England should relate to the works at Kirkby near Liverpool. On this site, which has now disappeared beneath a large housing estate, there was a major accident which was censored at the time but which would have been much worse had it not been for the heroic actions of one man. On 22nd February 1944 a group of women workers were filling anti-tank fuses when one exploded and ignited many others. One poor girl was literally blown to pieces and another two badly injured, one fatally. Arthur Bywater evacuated the badly damaged building and he then removed all the remaining fuses to a safe place. It was later found that he had removed no fewer than 12,724 fuses. For his bravery he was awarded both the George Cross and the George Medal. He was the only civilian to be given this dual award. Arthur Bywater spent his retirement in Australia and died in 2005 at the age of 91. Brave deeds by civilians have not always received the publicity which they deserved.

Chapter 5

Vickers Armstrong Under Fire

One of the best-kept secrets of the Second World War concerned the development of midget submarines. The Vickers Armstrong shipyard at Barrow-in-Furness was involved in this project. The works had specialised in the building of submarines prior to the First World War and during the Second World War, 99 of these vessels were launched. On one occasion a new submarine was launched on two successive days.

At this period the docks were being subjected to heavy bombing, as Geoff Cain, who worked in the Vickers yard and now lives at Penny Bridge near Ulverston, recalls:

> There were four Fire Watch and ARP control posts around the Works, each with a lookout on one of the tower cranes. Our lookout was on the 250-ton giant hammer head crane at Devonshire Dock. Sadly this crane is no more. It was a fine piece of civil engineering, built by the Sir William Arrol Company just before the war. When the German bombing raids began on London, Liverpool, Glasgow and other

cities and towns in 1940, we in Barrow often had air raid warnings. At first we dutifully went down to the office basement at work or, if at home, we sheltered under the stairs or in the brick shelters in the street. But there were so many false alarms that after a while we just did not bother. Some pundits used to theorise that the bombers could not find Barrow because of our geographical position under the lee of Black Combe.

We had the odd bombs of course, but in May 1941 they found Barrow all right and we had a week of heavy

The 250-ton crane at Devonshire Dock.

bombing raids. There was a fair amount of damage on a Sunday night. I was on fire duty at the Works. I was wearing my 'fire watcher's hat'. It was normal to do a four-hour watch but that night my mate Jim Silvie and I volunteered to do the full eight-hour watch on the 250-ton crane.

Access to the crane was forbidden during working hours but there was no nightshift on that night so we were able to roam all over the crane right up to the jockey crane on the top. We collected our rations and climbed the crane to the roller path some 150 feet above the dockside. On the roller path on the dockside there was a wooden hut with bunks and a telephone connected to the Control Post below.

The rations consisted of sandwiches and pork pies. The pies were wartime standard and not very appetising. We usually ended up dropping them down on the warships fitting out below and listening to the booming noise they made as they hit the decks. We thought it was all great fun.

It must have been about midnight when the air raid sirens sounded. We were not bothered after so many false alarms. But then the searchlights came on. They formed a ring around Barrow and we appeared to be in the middle, stuck up in the air like a bull's-eye. Then the incendiaries began to fall and it was not fun any more.

We had to report any incidents to the Control Post and give their bearings. To do this there was a simple plane table on the landward side of the roller path with a movable sighting arm that you could direct at the incident and read off the compass bearing. So we dashed to the plane table, took a bearing, dashed back to the hut and rang up Control.

'Stick of incendiaries dropped in the town near Buccleuch Street Power Station, bearing south-west.'

'Hang on while we plot it on the map.' Pause. 'That bearing puts the incident on Walney Island. Go and check again.'

So we went back to the plane table and realised in our panic that we had read the wrong end of the sighting arm. We should have given the bearing north-east. We were on our way back to the telephone to give them the correct bearing when the bomb fell. Conventional bombs make an unmistakable whistling noise as they fall. This one, as far as I remember, did not make any noise and Jim told me afterwards he had not heard anything either. There was talk at that time of parachute bombs which fell silently. Maybe it was one of those. But whatever it was, some primitive instinct alerted us and we flung ourselves face down on the plating of the roller path. I landed with my eyes looking down through a gap in the plating and I saw the bomb explode in a massive fireball on the Copper Shop at the foot of the crane. Mercifully no one was working in the shop that night.

Our little hut had been picked up and shaken like a child's toy and the telephone was out of action. In retrospect it would have been good to have stayed and watched the raid but we were far too scared to stay and we decided to get down to safety. How we got down in the dark I do not know. When we went back in the morning we found the access ladder down and the handrails which left the roller path on the landward side of the crane were all twisted and broken with the blast. Jim and I reported to the Control Post. John Warwick who was in charge said he had not expected to see us again.

The Luftwaffe obviously knew about the Barrow Yard and its reputation and the Germans had lots of relevant maps. They tried hard to bomb the works but they may well have been more determined had they known the details of one very secret project.

'X' class midget submarines were ordered by the Admiralty in great secrecy and with feverish urgency. It was the Barrow-built X5, X6, X7, X8, X9 and X10 submarines which in September 1943 successfully put the battleship *Tirpitz* out of action when she

An 'X' type midget submarine under trial.

was lying in the AltenFjord in Norway. All these small submarines had to be built and carefully tested under great secrecy by hand-picked civilian engineers, who were also closely involved during the sea trials. The classic film *Above Us the Waves* starring John Mills had Donald Cameron, VC, RNR, as its advisor. Cameron visited Barrow and worked alongside the civilian workers before himself leading the raid.

As was the case with the Royal Ordnance Factory at Chorley, there were some industrial disputes during the war but these were kept out of the news by the censor. With regards to shipbuilding in general and Barrow in particular, this has led some authors to exaggerate the facts. Some historians have suggested that the Vickers yard was often at a standstill, that very few ships were built and workers were either asleep or playing cards. The production figures do not, however, support these statements and politically biased observers in the 1990s should not be allowed to cast a slur on how hard these civilians at war did actually work during the 1940s.

Interior of the midget submarine.

In addition to the 99 submarines, this Vickers yard also constructed 4 aircraft carriers, 12 destroyers and 2 cruisers, which together totalled 109,628 tons. Eight of what became known as Empire Ships were also constructed, together weighing 59,078 tons. These were merchant ships of heavy construction capable of withstanding greater than normal damage and having cranes mounted on their superstructure which allowed quicker loading and unloading of cargo. This development was ideal when vessels were entering ports which had been badly damaged. These Empire vessels could also function as troop carriers. In addition, and under a high degree of secrecy, the Barrow yard constructed 25 landing craft and barges, some of which were used in the Normandy landings.

This does not suggest a lazy or an idle workforce and the Lancashire men and women who built ships should be given an honourable mention in the annals of the Second World War.

Chapter 6

Camouflage and Starfish

Ever since history began the arts of ambushing the enemy or hiding from them have been amongst the main strategies of war. It was only a small advance from an individual in concealment to the camouflage of weapons, but during the Second World War this was developed into sophisticated techniques to disguise buildings, factory complexes and even towns.

Some of Lancashire's cotton mills were commissioned to produce camouflage netting, as Barbara Mottram of Rochdale remembered:

> I was 12 or 13 at the time and every Saturday morning I volunteered to work in an old mill in Rochdale and we made camouflage netting. It was a dirty, dusty and tedious job, but parents encouraged us to do our bit for the war. We were involved in threading long strips of khaki, green, grey and brown material into netting which was hung from the mill ceilings. The heights of these sheds, as we called them, were ideal for this purpose. Some of us were perched on high ladders doing the top half whilst others worked on

the lower half. What the modern health and safety people would think of our elevated positions I shudder to think. It was a worthwhile job no doubt and when you see old films depicting battles all over the world showing gun emplacements, I wonder if I and my friends made any of this camouflage netting. We were well paid because we sometimes got a bag of sweets to share and these were not deducted from our rations.

Camouflage was not just for fighting in foreign fields. Lots of the netting was used locally, as with the threat of invasion pillboxes were built in their hundreds around the county. Many still remain and some historians feel that these should now be made listed buildings. Today the grey gaunt buildings stand out clearly in the landscape. This was not the case during the war. Each pillbox was

Many pillboxes have now been demolished, including the one on Pendle Hill. This photograph, including their Burnley hosts, was taken in 1946 when a group of refugees from Guernsey were reunited with their husbands.

camouflaged to fit in with the environment. Some in towns were made to resemble houses whilst others were surrounded by trees, but care was taken not to interfere with the line of fire. The impression these days is that a pillbox was just a block of crude concrete, which is far from the truth.

The roof was solid and the walls were composed of two layers. The outside was concrete but the inner skin was made of brick and between the two were strengthening wires. This design aimed at deflecting missiles whilst allowing fire to be directed out of five of the six sides. The sixth side was smaller and composed of a very solid metal door, which was well concealed. The camouflage was often imaginative as Sid Wilkes, who was a postman in the Lake District, recalls:

> Some pillboxes were in fields and were changed according to the season. I saw haystacks, storehouses for old ploughs and one was got up to look like a large harvesting machine complete with rust. There were lots of small belts of trees with one looking like a rookery and another one was embedded in a rose garden which was worth walking miles to see.

Many pillboxes for obvious reasons were positioned at railway road junctions, river crossings and anywhere that could control a bottleneck of invading traffic. There remains a fascinating pillbox controlling the crossing of the River Lune at Kirkby Lonsdale and almost astride the modern A65 road. These days it stands in splendid isolation on top of a hill but it would have been impossible to see if camouflaged to blend with the trees leading up to it.

There was an important pillbox towards the summit of Pendle Hill which was concealed in a fold of an artificial hill and doubled as a post for the Royal Observer Corps. Although this pillbox has been demolished, the concrete base on which it stood remains as a small car park leading up to the Nick of Pendle from the village of Sabden. This area was used to store munitions

A pillbox still in situ, which guarded the crossroads between Burnley Colne and Hebden Bridge.

which were dug into the ground and the pillbox was designed to protect these secret locations. There is no better camouflage than earth covered in grass and reed. Marlene Jaques remembers this pillbox very well:

> We had refugees from Guernsey in the Channel Isles staying with us during the war. The family we helped became friends and the women were worried about their men folk who did not get away. In 1946 the men came to visit us and we all went up onto Pendle and had our photographs taken by the pillbox. It was a different feeling to watch the reactions of the men who knew what it was like to be under Nazi occupation. They would have loved to have shot back! The Channel Islanders looked out over the Lancashire countryside and we pointed out Blackpool Tower which was at that time a real symbol of peace.

fashionable in recent years to suggest that the Dambusters' raid had 'little effect'. It should, however, not be forgotten that the dam breaches prevented the German armaments industries from functioning properly for several months. This seriously affected the Nazi war effort. Roy Chadwick, the designer of the Lancaster, was given credit for the achievement; Barnes Wallis, who created the bouncing bomb, sent him a letter to this effect and he was also awarded a CBE for his work.

In some cases serious efforts were made to camouflage whole factories, as was the case with the Royal Ordnance Factory at Chorley. Because of the explosives contained in the factory, units were built partly underground and all were covered in several feet of soil and seeded with grass and flowers. Around the flat areas, overlooked by moorland, false hillocks with dummy railway lines close by were created which must have been a problem for German navigators who already had difficulties negotiating the uplands.

The vulnerable docks of Manchester and Liverpool were targets for the German bombers and some camouflage defences were attempted. These strategies were employed all over Britain and were initially known as 'Special Fires', the idea being to light fires in safe areas which resembled burning around a vulnerable site. Later, Special Fire became abbreviated to 'Starfish'.

Navigation techniques on both sides were rudimentary and pathfinder aircraft dropped incendiaries to mark the target. At night, with lights in the right places, the remote Crown Point above Burnley could resemble Manchester under attack whilst Parbold Hill near Liverpool was a Starfish project well worth the small effort required to produce it and thus protect the docks.

The Starfish project meant persuading the enemy to drop their bombs in the wrong place, but other strategies involved building factories which appeared from the air to be something completely different. On Lake Windermere, for example, two almost identical factories were purpose-built during the war. They were, however, completely different in function.

One prominent factory was built to process perch which were sold under the attractive sounding title of Perchines in tomato

TELEGRAMS: "VICASTRONG-TELEX. WEYBRIDGE"
TELEPHONE : BYFLEET 240 (14 LINES)

REGISTERED OFFICE : VICKERS HOUSE
BROADWAY. WESTMINSTER. S.W.1.

Vickers-Armstrongs Limited.
(AIRCRAFT SECTION)

WEYBRIDGE WORKS.

WEYBRIDGE. SURREY.

OUR REF. CA.

YOUR REF.

25th May 1943.

Roy Chadwick, Esq.,
A.V.Roe & Co. Ltd.,
Greengate,
Middleton,
MANCHESTER

My dear Chadwick,

I am so sorry that my erratic movements since the great event have prevented my receiving your telegram of congratulations until today. I am very deeply grateful, but feel that an enormous share of the credit is due to you, and I have been trying to find the time to write and tell you how much I appreciate all the work which you and your assistants have done, and to congratulate you all on the immense success of your efforts. To you personally, in a special degree, was given the making or breaking of this enterprise, for if, at that fateful meeting in C.R.D's office on the 26th February, you had declared the task impossible of fulfilment in the given time, the powers of opposition were so great that I should never have got instructions to go ahead. Possibly you did not realise how much hung on your instantaneous reaction, but I can assure you that I very nearly had heart failure until you decided to join in the great adventure. No-one believed that we should do it. You yourself said it would be a miracle if we did, and I think the whole thing is one of the most amazing examples of team work and co-operation in the whole history of the war.

May I offer you my very deep thanks for the existence of your wonderful Lancaster, for it was the only aircraft in the world capable of doing the job, and I should like to pay my tribute of congratulation and admiration to you, the designer.

Let us hope that the future will hold for us another terrific adventure in which we may join, though I fear no such spectacular target remains to be brought down.

All good wishes for the future success of Lancasters and Yorks.

Yours very sincerely,

B.N.Wallis.

The congratulatory letter sent to Roy Chadwick by Barnes Wallis.

During the Second World War, a factory was set up on Lake Windermere to can the perch, one of the most common fish in the lake.

sauce. I did actually eat this product as a seven year old and I can remember that it tasted like . . . tomato sauce! It did, however, make a pleasant change from whale meat or wartime sausages. Nearby was a similar looking factory but this constructed Sunderland flying boats under licence from Short Aircraft Company. These Sunderlands were built in small numbers and were used in sea reconnaissance. There is a rumour that after the war some of these aircraft were scuttled in Lake Windermere and during 2003 and 2004 serious efforts were made to locate them.

The Sunderland Windermere project obviously did not create so much interest as the retrieval of Donald Campbell's *Bluebird* from Coniston. It is something of a surprise to find that *Bluebird* had its origins in a wartime factory in Lancashire. This was the small Samlesbury Engineering Company situated close to 15th-century Samlesbury Hall and the large aircraft factory. The engineering site is now occupied by the Manor Gardens Garden Centre but some remnants of what was once a runway can still be seen. During the war damaged Beaufighters were brought here on 60 ft trailers during the night. They were repaired and some flew off to resume action whilst others travelled on the trailers rather than have these returned empty. Although it is not often realised, many women were employed in the Air Force Auxiliary as delivery pilots, of whom the most famous was Amy Johnson. Squires Gate at Blackpool was one of her regular contact points.

Beaufighters were made by the Bristol Aviation Company and are best defined as a twin-engined night fighter. From 1942 they were fitted with an interception radar system. There was a shadow factory at the Fairey Aviation Works at Stockport producing standard Beaufighters. Why then send some aircraft to a small engineering works at Samlesbury? It may well have been at this insignificant location that the new radar systems were installed. Beaufighters played an important role in the Pacific War. Some were built in Australia and the Japanese referred to these fighters as

Sunderland flying boats were constructed at White Cross Bay on the shores of Windermere.

*A Bristol Beaufighter. Was the 'Whispering Death' just repaired at
Samlesbury Engineering, or was it secretly fitted with
new radar equipment there?*

'Whispering Death', so efficient were the 1,400 horse-power Bristol
Hercules engines!

Another secret factory was sited at Barton airfield on the
outskirts of Manchester where Merlin-engined Hawker Hurricanes
were adapted to be fitted onto the decks of merchant vessels. When
these ships were attacked by long-range German aircraft the
Hurricane was launched via a catapult and could wreak havoc
against the slow moving and comparatively poorly armed
bombers. The trip for the Hurricanes was, however, one way
because there was no space to land on the deck of a merchantman.
The pilot therefore circled the host ship and landed on the sea to be
picked up by lifeboat. The Air Ministry was prepared to sacrifice
one aircraft which could not be recovered from the sea but which
had destroyed one, two or even three much larger and more
expensive long-range bombers. The Germans might lose fifteen
aircrew whilst the British pilot was safely retrieved. There was only
one side which could be the victor in this economic and manpower
battle.

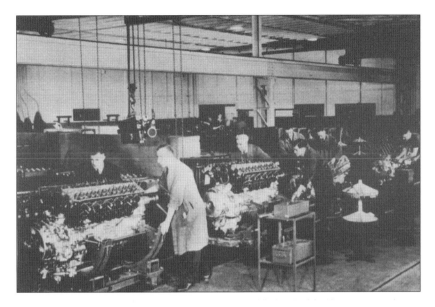

Rolls-Royce Merlin engines being assembled at the old Ford factory in Eccles. Shadow factories were vital to prevent one bombing raid bringing all production of a vital commodity to a halt.

Military facilities were also disguised. At Brungerley Bridge, near Clitheroe, the Royal Engineers spent time training troops on the art of bridge building. Some of their concrete emplacements remain and can be seen on the banks of the River Ribble and alongside the well-used footpath.

The Royal Engineers, should the occasion have arisen, would not only have been able to build bridges but also to have destroyed the substantial Brungerley Bridge and many others in the region. The troops were billeted in the hamlet of Low Moor and the local church has a hatchment commemorating their presence. It is 'probable' that the officers and 'other important workers' had their headquarters at the nearby Little Mitton Hall, dating to the 14th century and which is now a restaurant.

The presence of these units was kept low key, but there was a completely opposite strategy and this was to pretend that an installation was more important than it actually was. Many golf courses suddenly sprouted posts, some of which were placed to resemble gun emplacements, which would deter any airborne landings and direct aircraft towards the real anti-aircraft guns which were much more skilfully camouflaged. Malcolm Haydock remembers well one of these emplacements at Pleasington Golf Course near Blackburn: 'As a youngster I wondered why all this was necessary especially as some of the old golfers complained about all the obstructions sprouting on the fairway. The better players smiled and pointed out that those who did most of the complaining never hit the fairways anyway!'

These high profile tactics were on a very minor scale compared to one of the largest and most successful confidence tricks carried out during the war. The Knutsford area, just in Cheshire but close to Manchester, became the headquarters of General George Patton, the flamboyant American commander, in early 1944 as part of the deception plan prior to the Normandy invasion. The Germans became convinced that Patton's troops would spearhead the invasion from his base here in the North-West and that the attack would be concentrated around Calais and certainly not on Normandy. 'Secret' documents were deliberately allowed to be leaked and the Germans certainly fell for the ruse. Thousands of workmen from the Manchester area were bussed daily into the Tatton area to build the accommodation supposedly for thousands of GIs. Most of the constructions were merely shells and the relatively few troops who were posted there were told to keep busy moving about. 'Munitions' were delivered daily and the telephones were kept humming. Patton did not like being used as a mere decoy but the ruse succeeded and thousands of German troops remained idle in the Calais area thinking that the Normandy invasion was just a diversion. This saved thousands of Allied lives.

Alex Murray who was a carpenter recalls that local people were taken in as well:

> Lots of buildings were under construction around a large area of countryside and as very few were finished we all

thought that the invasion of Europe would be as late as 1946. We were all surprised after Normandy to realise that it was a massive con trick and that Patton's Army was a ruse. I'm sure that a lot that went on in the war was just a ruse but I was pleased to be one of the blind men helping to bluff Adolf.

General Patton moved into Peover Hall and dined at the Whipping Stocks Hotel. When he went overseas just prior to D-Day he left money to ensure that fresh flowers were provided to decorate his favourite table for a year. This tradition is maintained to the present day.

Chapter 7

Keeping the Water Flowing

These days the water supply for the whole of the North-West is under the control of United Utilities but in 1939 each town had its own water supply complete with reservoirs and piping. During the war the waterworks staff, often in association with the Home Guard, had the job of protecting this vital resource. Each reservoir had to be guarded and the keepers of the waters also had to be aware of their duties should an invasion force try to interfere with water supplies. If normal water supplies should be disrupted and bombing caused fires, plans had to be made to draw water directly from nearby canals and rivers. These watercourses were marked on maps and also had to be protected and this accounts for the position of many pillboxes.

It would seem that the water companies were better prepared than most other industries as the storm clouds of war began to gather. As early as 1936 the Preston Waterworks reacted by combining with a number of smaller works nearby. The aim was to provide mutual aid in the event of a terrorist attack or an invasion. Meetings were held regularly and staff volunteered to do three

*During the Blitz, water often ran out or pipes were damaged.
In each town and city, as here in Manchester, maps were made
locating emergency supplies from canals, rivers
and even old mill ponds.*

nights' watch duty, three nights on standby and six nights free on a roster basis. The partnership purchased fire pumps, reserve water, piping, rations, clothing and even specially adapted vehicles. Practice runs were organised and particular emphasis was placed on anticipating the risk of sabotage. Patrols were organised and two 'formidable' bull mastiffs were purchased.

Some other innovations were triggered by the war and in 1940 a water laboratory was established at Longridge. For the first time tests were routinely made for chemical and bacteriological contamination. Enemy activities made it necessary to treat the water with chlorine to ensure that the water remained fit for consumption. Minute doses of chlorine were already used but the concentration was substantially increased, as any damage by 'hostile individuals' would obviously contaminate supplies. The belief was that if extra chlorine was added as a routine then any contaminant introduced by the enemy would be neutralised.

Apart from individuals causing damage there was the possibility of bomb damage to the piping. Until the Dambusters' raid on the Ruhr Valley in 1943 neither side had the capability of dropping a bomb of sufficient accuracy or size to destroy a dam; a single bomb, however, could accidentally fracture an important mains pipe. The Preston area somehow missed the main blitz and its 200 miles of piping remained intact. One bomb did land close to Stone Cross at Grimsargh but did not explode. It was, however, perilously close to a 36 inch main and this was dealt with by a brave UXB (UneXploded Bomb) crew.

One night the workers of the Water Company watched what they described as a 'stick of bombs' drop in the area but little damage was done, as the Divisional Manager, W. Yale, recalled: 'We all made a (more or less) dignified retreat to the protection of the valve house as the bombs sounded nearer and nearer, each trying not to be the last man in. We had many alerts and we made many an eerie journey with no lights through the blackout at all hours of the night to inspect the various works.' There was a wartime direction to keep supplies running with minimal costs but once hostilities ceased 'make do' had to be changed to 'replace all worn out services'.

Some areas of the region were more vulnerable than others. Liverpool's water supply came by pipeline from North Wales and from the Rivington area around Darwen and Bolton, while two long underground pipelines, one from the Derbyshire area and the other from the Lake District, provided water to Manchester. Both the latter were, and still are, magnificent examples of Victorian engineering expertise but they were obviously not designed to resist attack.

Prior to 1851, Manchester's water supply was unreliable both in quantity and quality. The idea of a pipeline running 18 miles eastwards to Manchester from the Longdendale Valley, along the Pennine Chain into Derbyshire, was ambitious. A string of reservoirs were constructed by damming the local rivers, mainly the Etherow and Goyt, which are the major tributaries of the

All reservoirs had to be protected during the war. Here at Hurstwood, near Burnley, there were lots of areas which could conceal those up to no good. The local Home Guard patrolled the old lead workings seen in the background.

*Control towers like this one at Hurstwood Reservoir were vulnerable
to attack and were guarded.*

Mersey. The water flowed through a pipe by the force of gravity to
the city. All these plans involved cutting through land purchased
from Sir Oswald Mosley, the then lord of the manor of Manchester
and whose son of the same name was to become the most
notorious fascist in Britain. Hitler's plan for a defeated Britain was
to restore Edward VIII to the throne and install Oswald Mosley as
a puppet political leader. Mosley's sympathy for the Nazis meant
that the enemy would have access to a detailed knowledge of these
vulnerable water pipelines.

From the late 1870s, when the expanding city of Manchester was
short of water, a new pipeline to the Lake District was planned.
After a great deal of negotiation the Thirlmere scheme became
operational from 12th October 1894. The publicity was such that
the route of the gravity-fed pipeline was well known and so were
the locations of treatment works and major branching points
where water was fed to towns. As the storm clouds built up in the

The Metro-Vickers factory in Manchester constructed mobile power stations capable of generating 2,500 kilowatts.

1930s plans had to be made to guard more than 90 miles of vulnerable pipeline. It is known that German Intelligence had copies of these water pipeline schemes and also those serving the Fylde through the Trough of Bowland.

It was not just water supplies which had to be protected. Under a cloak of secrecy the Metro-Vickers factory in Trafford Park, Manchester produced, among other things, mobile power stations which could be transported on huge trucks and were capable of generating up to 2,500 kilowatts of electricity when required.

Gas works and the piping which linked them to consumers were also vulnerable, as retired Manchester policeman Dennis Wood told me:

> Each copper at this time went on duty with a rifle and five rounds of ammunition and kept an eye open for saboteurs around power stations, gas works, telephone exchanges and other areas regarded as vulnerable. The man on the beat worked closely with the Home Guard and the Air Raid Wardens. Obviously there was not a lot the Bobby could do

when a bomb fell but it was essential to report any damage as soon as possible.

The Police Museum in Manchester has a record of officers' notebooks written up whilst on duty during this period.

Many of the Home Guard who would have defended these essential supplies were trained at the Altcar camp situated on the coast between Liverpool and Southport. Altcar, which still functions today and is run by the Territorial Army, has a long and distinguished history. It developed because of a much earlier invasion threat.

In 1859 one of Napoleon's descendants threatened to invade England, perhaps via Ireland. If this happened then the Port of Liverpool would be most vulnerable and influential merchants set about establishing a Rifle Club with gentlemen members. This was set up by 1860 and the Altcar Range was funded by members and

A mobile transformer built by Ferranti at Trafford Park. It was used by the ARP to restore power to areas which had been bombed. Once repairs had been carried out, the transformer could be moved wherever it was needed. (Ferranti Archive)

not by the War Office, which was keen on the idea but never provided financial backing, except for the provision of ammunition during the two world wars. The Liverpool area therefore had a reservoir of marksmen able to shoot to a high standard using the latest weapons which they could well afford to purchase. Members won every competition on offer and at one time it was proposed that the national shooting competition should be held not at Bisley but at Altcar. At the start of the Second World War, Altcar was taken over for tank training and anti-aircraft guns were sited at the camp.

What happened also at the start of the war was an assault by old soldiers and marksmen on the War Office asking to be accepted for the armed forces. Many old officers from the First World War were turned down on the grounds of age and were not very pleased at the rejection. They became a thorn in the side of those organising the Home Guard. The solution seems to have been to swear the old lads to secrecy and form them into small groups with orders to lie low and wait. There is no doubt that these aged marksmen and their pieces of ancient but often sophisticated ordnance, besides those with modern rifles, would have accounted for quite a few Germans if they had invaded.

Chapter 8

Secrets of the Sea

Much has been written about the blitz of Liverpool with German bombers hammering away at the docks, which were literally heaving with shipping. Less, however, has been written about the U-boats and single aircraft that made their way into Liverpool Bay and laid thousands of magnetic mines on the shipping lanes leading to the docks. The mines were triggered by the very delicate changes in the magnetic fields between the metal hulls of the ships as they passed close to the mine, the natural chemicals in seawater and the design of the mine itself.

When it is realised that more than 70 vessels arrived at Liverpool docks every day the threat posed by mines spread along the approaches can be appreciated. I gained an idea of the extent of the problem when I was commissioned by BBC Radio Merseyside to write and present a series of programmes called *The Wrecks of Liverpool Bay*. When I began to research the subject I was expecting to find evidence of sailing ships, perhaps loaded with valuables including gold, sunk by storm and this was indeed the case, but I was also given access to maps of the seabed of Liverpool

Bay on which were marked wrecks and other hazards. At this point I had a great surprise as I could see marked the submerged wrecks of vessels sunk by mines during Second World War.

The *Munster*, built by Harland and Wolff in Belfast in 1938, was sunk by a mine on 7th February 1940. This caused a great controversy, as it was the most important passenger ferry between England and Ireland, but to the Naval authorities the loss of one relatively small passenger ferry operating from the North-West of England was nothing compared to the massive losses of merchant vessels carrying vital supplies. Between December 1939 and June 1940, 2.3 million tons of shipping were lost. This figure increased to 2.5 million tons from July to December 1940 and to 2.9 million tons in the period from January 1941 to June 1941. The Germans had correctly calculated that if they could sink merchant vessels faster than they could be built then they would win the war. Oil tankers were obviously a prime target because Britain was totally reliant upon foreign fuel supplies.

The crews of merchant ships, which had already braved the seas and the U-boats in the Atlantic, must have considered themselves terribly unlucky to be sunk by mine when they thought that they

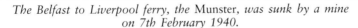

The Belfast to Liverpool ferry, the Munster, *was sunk by a mine on 7th February 1940.*

The oil tanker El Oso *at her berth (above) and being devastated by a mine on 17th January 1940.*

were home and almost (quite literally) dry. Included among the ships lost in this manner were the tanker *El Oso*, the cargo vessel *Cairross* (17th January 1940) and MV *Charges* (9th February 1940). I spoke to 91-year-old Jimmy Flynn who was a seaman for 40 years and on convoy duty out of Liverpool. He was sunk twice and he told me:

Them in the Merchant Navy got a raw deal. Nearly 30% of my mates did not survive the war. We were not pleased when we found out that our pay was stopped the minute the cargo was lost. Them who died got no money and nowt was paid to their widows or kids. Some of us worked out how much we got paid per hour and compared our wages with them working in the docks or in armament factories. I still loved the sea despite the danger. It was okay when the weather was rough and even when we were under attack because then we had no time to think. But we did get talking with our mates when the sea was calm and we were safe. This is when we realised that we had a bloody raw deal. Most of us who were mined or torpedoed and survived soon found another ship. We were gluttons for punishment, don't you think?

The large transatlantic convoy vessels were not the only ships to be operating to and from Liverpool. The coastal trade was essential during the war. These small vessels allowed the various ports around Britain to keep contact with each other, and with the road, rail and canal systems all under pressure the coasters were vital to move goods around. Liverpool was an important link because goods from North America and beyond could be unloaded from large vessels to the coasters. Many of these small vessels were sunk by mines, including the *Gorsethorn* sunk on 8th December 1940, the *Ystroom* sunk on 23rd December 1940 and the *Calcium*, which slipped beneath the waves of Liverpool Bay on 30th December 1940.

The Royal Navy needed answers and they needed them in a hurry. They had experimented with their own version of a magnetic mine from the 1920s but had made very little progress in what they misguidedly regarded as a low priority project. They now not only needed to develop their own weapon but more importantly they needed to know how to neutralise such a device!

What Britain needed was a stroke of luck and fortunately this was not long in coming. In 1940 a German seaplane dropped magnetic mines around the Thames estuary and two fell in very soft mud and failed to explode. A team of brave bomb disposal officers dismantled them, made drawings of the parts and analysed the workings. This gave a clue how to neutralise these mines.

The boffins evolved a technique which became known as 'degaussing'. In its simplest form this meant passing a calculated amount of electric current through cables across the hull of the vessel. This effectively cancelled out the ship's own electrical field and any nearby magnetic mine failed to detonate. Elsie Whiteside worked at Waterside Mill in Bury where a special fabric was woven for covering the cables used in the degaussing of ships. Elsie recalls: 'We were not used to producing this strange cloth but we were told that it had to do with army webbing. It was only after the war that I was told it went either to Liverpool or Fleetwood to be fitted to ships.'

Other devices constructed in Lancashire factories included depth charge throwers, which hurled the devices from the rear of ships. The Royal Navy also developed a secret weapon which was called the 'Hedgehog'. This fired a salvo of bombs forward, which exploded over a wider area and did much more damage than a conventional depth charge. Statistics released after the war note that depth charge successes were never greater than 7% but Hedgehog attacks sometimes reached what was known as a 'kill rate' of 25%.

Another anti-mine precaution was to adapt vessels made of wood to carry out minesweeping operations. Fishing trawlers were considered to be ideal for this purpose. By the late 1930s the Admiralty had a list of trawlers and also of their skippers based in all the fishing ports, including Fleetwood. Names like Harrison, Stock, Wignall and the Wrights (Slippy and Toby) were high on the lists of wanted men.

In September 1939 most of Fleetwood's trawlers became His Majesty's ships. The Lago Company had a dozen well-equipped trawlers and in one stroke of the pen all had been taken over by the Navy. There was a communication forewarning the company who recalled all trawlers at sea and those about to sail were kept in

The Sierra, *built as a whaler in 1929 but converted for minesweeping in 1940.*

port. The Marr Company also gave up their ships and they had 21 vessels based in Fleetwood plus a smaller fleet of eight operating out of Hull.

By the Fall of Dunkirk in 1940 there were only two trawlers landing fish at Fleetwood and a number had already been sunk with the loss of many lives. Still obviously classed as civilians, the ultimate sacrifice made by the trawler men has never been fully recognised apart from in the fishing ports themselves. Many vessels just 'disappeared' and it was only after the war when the U-boat and Luftwaffe combat reports could be examined that the fate of these trawlers could be confirmed and the families of those involved officially told. Some trawlers were not considered by U-boat commanders to be worth a valuable torpedo and their skippers surfaced and sank the unarmed fishing vessels with gunfire. Those trawlers engaged in minesweeping would not have carried guns made of metal in the early years of the war as that would have reduced the degaussing defences of the ship. The Marr vessels the *Lord Minto* and the *Arlita* were sunk by gunfire whilst they were actually fishing off the Flannan Islands in September 1939. They had no guns of their own.

Obviously, because of the importance of food some fishing had to go on but the trawlers operating out of Hull and Grimsby were in greater danger because they were closer to the continent. Thus Fleetwood became the major fishing port during the war; fish, because it was difficult to keep prior to us having freezers and refrigerators, was not rationed but was available if and when it arrived. Potatoes were not rationed either and fish and chip shops therefore remained open throughout the war. If fish was not available then chips, peas and gravy with pickled onions could be bought.

In a move kept very secret the East Coast ports sent out their trawlers ostensibly to the fishing grounds but they were then diverted to Fleetwood to be fitted out as minesweepers. More often than not only the skippers knew of the true destination and the crew were only informed whilst at sea.

Some East Coast trawlers had naval personnel put on board just before sailing and one such was His Majesty's Trawler (HMT) *Northern Gem* which sailed out of Grimsby. One of the officers was Jim Pooley of Fleetwood, and some of the 'deckies' were also Fleetwood lads. For the first time since the First World War the fishermen all worked together and inter-port rivalries were forgotten.

HMT *Northern Gem* was one of 15 vessels of the same design which were requisitioned by the Admiralty, which is somewhat ironic because they were all built in Germany in 1936. Each vessel, much larger than its English equivalents, was 655 tonnes in weight and the crew accommodation was described as 'luxurious'. Luxurious is a term which I think is best considered as comparative. With the exception of the *Northern Princess,* all vessels of this class survived the war. One wonders if their German appearance may have confused the enemy, but as with many aspects of the secret war we will never know!

The fact remains, however, that the almost (but not quite) crippling losses of the Fleetwood trawlers serving as both

The Northern Gem *was a German-built trawler operating out of Grimsby.
Taken over by the Navy, her crew included Jim Pooley of Fleetwood
(second from left). Many trawler men were incorporated into
the crews of the minesweepers.*

minesweepers and fishing vessels was a sad but proud chapter in the history of the port. In the first three months of the war, the Fleetwood fishing fleet was depleted by seven and the families of 37 men were left penniless; like the rest of the merchant service there was no pay from the minute the vessel began to sink.

The trawler men were angry that they could not fight back. 'It was bad enough being bloody well shot at,' recalled William Gunson, 'and at the very least we wanted to shoot back.' The Admiralty eventually responded by secretly sending trawler men to Liverpool where they were trained to operate a gun fitted with degaussing equipment and which was mounted aft of the vessel. The men were trained to Royal Navy standards but retained their civilian status.

Another 'secret' use of the Fleetwood trawlers and those from the East Coast ports was during the evacuation of Dunkirk. Arthur Lewis, the skipper of the steam trawler *Evelyn Rose*, returned from fishing off Iceland late on a Saturday night. The catch was quickly unloaded on the Sunday, which was an almost unheard of situation, and the skipper was given sealed and secret orders and set off to sea with the same crew. He was ordered to go to Plymouth where he was met by a very junior naval officer who was only present as a gesture. Arthur Lewis remained skipper even though the White Ensign flag was replaced by the Red Ensign of the Royal Navy. He was given charts and told to proceed to Dunkirk. Here the *Evelyn Rose* took on board 317 soldiers and after landing them safely he returned to the beaches via Ramsgate and took off around 400 more men.

Other Fleetwood trawler skippers were given the same secret orders and the *Velia*, *Edwina*, *Dhoon* and *Jacinta* also braved the beaches at Dunkirk. Mention must also be made of skipper Arthur Day and his vessel *Gava* which operated under the control of the Naval Patrol Service, more of which later in this chapter. Three of the crew were decorated for the part they played in the rescue from the sea of some wounded French troops whilst themselves coming under heavy fire from German aircraft including Stukas. The sound of these dive-bombers was designed to instil fear. These three

Fleetwood lads, named as Dunne, Gawne and Jones, braved this terror.

Fleetwood not only played host to East Coast trawlers but also welcomed foreign visitors. As the Nazis occupied Europe many fishermen, especially from Holland, Belgium and Denmark decided to 'disappear'. Many men and their vessels eventually ended up in Fleetwood where the crews were initially accommodated in the British Legion Club. All were made welcome and one vessel in particular proved to be a real bonus. This was the *Vestland* and crewman Otto Jensen has vivid memories of this period. She was only commissioned in 1937 and was at that time the largest Danish seine netter ever built and had an overall length of 85 feet.

Many of these 'foreign' fishermen realised what was about to happen as war broke out and some managed to smuggle their families on board but Otto Jensen had no such luck. He recalls:

> On the 7th April 1940 we sold our catch at Grimsby and as we were about to return home the news came that the Germans had invaded and occupied my home port of Esbjerg which was then sealed. Even before we left Denmark, German gunboats were in evidence but our skipper managed to steer clear of them. After being kept waiting a week or so we were told to sail to Fleetwood and we fished there throughout the war. We made lifelong friends with the local folk. When fishing is in your blood, language does not matter.

There is no doubt that the delay at Grimsby was to ensure that all the crew were vetted to prevent German agents infiltrating the British merchant fleet.

Jensen is a common name in Denmark and Victor Jensen was also pleased to be sailing, as he put it, 'under the British flag rather than cringing under the German jackboot. Our ship was called the *Iceland* and at first it was taken over by the British Navy but later on our own skipper was put back in charge but the crew was broken up. I had to make a living and soon got a berth with a ship

The two Danes, Victor and Otto Jensen, revisiting Fleetwood to remember their time here in the 1940s.

called *Mackenzie II*. I stayed with this ship all through the war and we fished out of Iceland. The Fleetwood folk always made us welcome.'

A great deal has obviously been written about the Royal Navy during the war but hardly anything about the trawlermen, and even less about the Royal Naval Patrol Service. This can very loosely be described as bridging the gap between the two. Charles Stewart of Blackpool told me that:

> At the start of the war the RNPS consisted of skippers, mates and men of the Royal Naval Reserve and initially there were 6,000 men and 600 vessels which could be called upon. At the end of the war 60,000 men and 6,000 vessels were in service. The men of the Royal Naval Patrol Service were trained at Lowestoft in a requisitioned municipal pleasure ground which became known as the Sparrow's Nest. The men were billeted with seaside landladies and referred to themselves as Harry Tate's Navy.

The Patrol Service did sterling work during the retreat of troops from the ill-fated Narvic sortie in Norway. The aim of that had been to prevent the rich iron ore fields of Norway from falling into German hands but the troops were insufficient in numbers and not equipped to fight in wintry conditions. During the withdrawal, fourteen trawlers were lost and many Fleetwood-based men of the RNPS died. At Dunkirk, 243 'trawler-type' vessels were in action and no fewer than 198 were sailing under the orders of the RNPS.

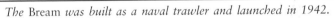

The Bream *was built as a naval trawler and launched in 1942.*

During the war 13,890 men from this proud service, still defined as 'Civilians at War', lost their lives. This represents a mortality rate of one in six.

It was not just the civilians who went to sea who should be celebrated here but those who worked in and around the docks also need to be remembered. As the Fleetwood trawlers were being adapted to serve as minesweepers the work carried on by James Robertson and Sons was very important. This engineering works situated on Dock Street in Fleetwood constructed degaussing equipment, depth charge throwers and winches among other things. All this equipment had to be produced to exact Admiralty specifications. I was able, thanks to the assistance of Simon Hayhow, the curator of Fleetwood Museum, to study the archives of James Robertson and Sons. I could examine all the relevant drawings, which proved how skilled the civilian workforce must have been. Here were breathtakingly complex (and then secret) drawings of winches built so that they operated without sparking. Winches for trawlers were provided and used in 25 vessels (numbered 1483 to 1508) – the grease nipples had to conform to Admiralty Pattern 4986 and even the oil used was specified as Admiralty Pattern 4531!

The activities of the RNPS were known to German Intelligence because of the bravery of the service but under the British blanket of security the details of their losses were not released. Because of this too few people know of the role these men played, save those who survived and those who mourned the deaths of comrades. It is hoped that the few lines set down here will provide an epitaph for those trawling families who lost loved ones in Grimsby, Hull, Lowestoft and, in the context of this book, in Fleetwood.

Chapter 9

If Invasion Comes

Since its history began, Britain has been a maritime country which could, until recently, only trade by sea. Being an island she could also use the sea as a barrier against invasion. The German use of massive air support meant that some change in strategy had to be contemplated. It was accepted that invasion would be instigated by paratroops backed up soon afterwards by waves of troops – a sort of Normandy in reverse. Whilst most attention was focused on the South-East coastline it was thought that there was still a very real threat of an invasion of the North-West of England via Ireland and perhaps also via the Isle of Man.

Plans to deal with a possible invasion were put in hand early in the war, when it was realised that different regions would need to have their own specific arrangements. The Dunkirk fiasco, or miracle, whichever way you look at it, showed that troop movements were hindered by the thousands of refugees carrying their belongings and blocking the roads. Confused people just moved without knowing where they were heading and the military became bogged down and totally incapacitated, so throughout

Even before the war the ARP services were trained to react to emergency situations. This happened in all towns, including as here at Barrow-in-Furness.

Britain civilians were told that they should stay put and await instructions. But what were these instructions and how did they apply to Lancashire? And what other restrictions were imposed on day-to-day life to counter the threat?

One answer can be found in an official document which was issued on 13th August 1942 under the heading *Invasion Preparations*, by the Regional Commissioner based at Arkwright House on Parsonage Gardens in Manchester. Only four copies were issued, extracts from which make fascinating reading. A Mr C.J. Bentley wrote:

I am directed by the Regional Commissioner to state that he is glad to note that progress has been made for the establishment of Invasion Conferences throughout the Region and that the deep interest of these authorities as custodians of the welfare of the Civic Population has been recognised by the appointment of their chief citizen or the chairman of an appropriate Committee of the Council as Chairman of the Invasion Conference.

The date of this document is interesting in the context of some shift of government opinion. With the RAF emerging victorious from the Battle of Britain the threat of invasion had disappeared. Or had it? Certainly the German plan of invading the South-East of England via the ports of France and Belgium was abandoned. However, there was still considered to be a threat of smaller invasions from Southern Ireland or by parachutists as aircraft became larger and their operational range increased. By 1942 these smaller scale invasions had to be expected and planned for and the document continues:

In most cases it is observed that the Conferences are proceeding on the lines which have been recommended vis: a small permanent nucleus to act as a co-ordinating body with an ad-hoc representation of other services when matters affecting them arise for discussion. The Invasion Conference is a planning body whose function it is to make arrangements beforehand. When the time comes for executive action under invasion conditions, the local military commander will wish to deal with one or two persons only on the civil side and the inner nucleus of the Invasion Conference should therefore be capable of functioning on the lines of a triumvirate with the police representative as the Civil Staff Officer and the chief citizen, chairman or mayor as the general representative of the civil side.

The document goes on to refer to a pamphlet dated July 1942, entitled *Consolidated Instructions to Invasion Committees*, which although couched in general terms provides for regional variations. This pamphlet was marked as top secret and could only be viewed by Military Commanders, Controllers of Civil Defence, the Senior Police Officer and the National Fire Service (which was instigated only in 1942) along with heads of 'certain' government departments. Broadly speaking, plans were made on two fronts. Firstly, the invasion must be repelled. Only if this failed was phase two to be put into operation, and this would have involved an organised resistance movement, which is described in a later chapter. The initial thrust of the pamphlet was that:

> If the enemy should invade this country, he must be driven out or destroyed as quickly as possible. The primary object of invasion preparations is to meet the military requirements and the well being of the civilian population must necessarily be a secondary consideration. Time will be short and the needs great. There must be the closest collaboration between the civil and the military authorities; and the civil authorities and the civil population must give all necessary assistance to the military authorities.

It was a directive which had changed little since 1939, when measures were immediately taken to control possible collaboration with the enemy and to make life as difficult as possible for any invading German.

Milestones and signposts had been removed all over England, while civilians were employed to paint out the names of railway stations or other signs which could help the enemy. So that the Invasion Committees would not themselves be confused the Ordnance Survey prepared detailed maps, but it also had to be assumed that the Germans had relevant maps and the staff who could read them. In the upland areas of North-West England, direction finding was not easy (and still isn't) but even so plans were made to produce confusing landmarks and set up indicators pointing in the wrong direction.

Lists were prepared of those British individuals who were likely to be sympathetic to the Germans. There were ardent fascists in Britain, including Sir Oswald Mosley, who as mentioned earlier was a local landowner and had many friends who thought that what Hitler was doing in Germany could and should be replicated in Britain. These lists remain secret to this day but there were plans to 'react to the threat posed by these people should invasion come'. What this actually meant was deliberately left vague!

Dennis Wood remembers Mosley speaking to a Manchester audience of several thousand at Heaton Park in 1937 – he had plenty of supporters but he was also heckled by a large group of Jewish Mancunians.

Another even more famous face – or voice – had Manchester connections and this was Lord Haw-Haw, alias William Joyce (1906–1946). Again Dennis Wood remembers that most laughed but a few were inspired:

> He broadcast in English during the Second World War from Germany, with the intention of inducing Great Britain to capitulate. Aged 17 he had joined the British Fascist Party, but left after two years and joined the Conservative Party. In spite of his gift as a speaker he was not encouraged by that party and he rejoined Sir Oswald Mosley's Fascists, becoming, within two years, his director of propaganda, but they quarrelled and Joyce founded his own British National Socialist League. Joyce had resided in Manchester before the war and was at that time arrested in connection with his speaking in such places as Stevenson Square in the city and trying to raise the crowd to overthrow the English Parliament and the Crown. He was detained in a cell at Newton Street Police Station (now the Greater Manchester Police Museum). In 1939 he disappeared from Britain, making his debut soon after as a broadcaster from Berlin. Throughout the war he spoke almost nightly warning the population of Britain as to which city was to be bombed that night, and he was often correct. He spoke on other subjects, often lying as to the fate of warships or troops in the various theatres of the war. There was a peculiar timbre in his voice which listeners were said to find fascinating.

After the collapse of Germany he was found hiding in a forest near the Danish frontier, and was recognised by his voice alone.

At the opposite end of the spectrum to these high-profile traitors were anarchists and communists who were also conscientious objectors. They too were listed and those not already in prison would have to be dealt with if invasion was imminent. Those Germans and Italians who had immigrated into Britain were interned on the Isle of Man although most were later released when it was discovered that they were loyal to their adopted country.

Care and an objective standpoint need to be taken of the loose term 'conscientious objectors'. The government and, especially, the police had to deal with two main areas of civil disobedience and the refusal of able-bodied men to fight. There were many brave men whose conscience prevented them from taking human life but who were prepared to serve as voluntary firemen, stretcher bearers or ambulance drivers, or to work down the coal mines. These men were respected far more than those whose political beliefs persuaded them that the existing democratic way of life in Britain had to be changed, perhaps in favour of communism. Such people were a danger to the war effort. Initially no distinction was made between these two categories and many conscientious objectors were jailed with a few extremists being shot.

The police obviously had a crucial role in the maintenance of law and order, but as invasion looked likely they were also urged to be vigilant in detecting what were defined as 'subversive or treacherous activities'.

The Independent Labour Party was one body targeted by the police as a hotbed for conscientious objectors. Between the villages of Newchurch and Roughlee, overlooked from Pendle Hill and close to the towns of Burnley and Nelson, is Clarion House. This still stands and is open especially on Sundays for walkers, some now well into their eighties and who still enjoy a brew, a butty and a talk. The Clarion was named after a Socialist weekly newspaper.

Clarion House near Nelson – the focus for conscientious objectors, most of whom were well meaning and no real threat to anyone.

There were, in the 1920s, several Clarion House 'snack bars-cum-meeting houses' but only the Nelson one has survived.

During the First World War many conscientious objectors had gathered there and anti-war meetings were held; police raids and arrests were frequent. For many years the town of Nelson was referred to as 'Little Moscow' and even in the 1950s Dick Bland, who had spent three years in prison during the First World War, had to resign as Mayor because he refused to meet the Queen if she had any form of military escort. It has to be admitted that many of the objectors were both stubborn and brave. They lost their jobs, were sent white feathers and were refused admission to shops, some public buildings and most pubs, although few ILP members were bothered about drink; many were lifelong abstainers. Even their families were persecuted and members spent their time with like-minded folk and worked at improving the facilities at Clarion House.

During the Second World War Clarion House offered hospitality to a group of Sudetan refugees who were the victims of the vicious Nazi regime. They were brought over as a result of the efforts of an Independent Labour Party member, John McNair. He fought for the Communists against the Fascists in the Spanish Civil War and would not fight for Britain but he was an able man who worked as an interpreter for General de Gaulle, who did not think much of Britain either! The Sudetans were housed at Hebden Bridge but were entertained several times at Clarion House.

The Independent Labour Party had proved to be too left wing even for the Labour Party in 1932 and there is no doubt that Clarion House was targeted by the police as they were ordered to rout out all objectors but particularly those regarded as Communist sympathisers. A lot of time, effort and money were spent pursuing men and some women who felt that they were being denied the right of free speech. Only a very small minority could have been regarded as much of a threat.

*   *   *

In the invasion plans the services of individual women and especially women's organisations were considered to be crucially important. Civilians and soldiers had to be fed and watered and accommodation had to be provided for people whose houses had been bombed or whose homes were requisitioned by the army for defence purposes. A billeting officer or officers was appointed for every city, district or small village. It is not well known that Lancashire played a major role in the organisation of billeting and the provision of rest centres, through the Women's Voluntary Service (WVS).

When Lady Reading was asked by the government to organise the Women's Voluntary Service in 1938 she used her connections with the Girl Guide movement and integrated this within a network of mature but influential ladies. One such was Rachael Kay-Shuttleworth of Gawthorpe Hall, near Burnley who became the very first member of the WVS movement in Lancashire. She was very proud of this membership number.

Rachael told me that it was immediately obvious to her that invasion via the North-West of England was possible and plans had to be drawn up not later but very much sooner. She set about talking to all Local Authorities in Lancashire and called many meetings – these were not to be talking shops but, during the deliberations, workable plans had to be laid down in writing. She realised that transport would be vital, especially in rural areas, and she made lists of

Rachael Kay-Shuttleworth (right) of Gawthorpe Hall did more than anyone to plan for the WVS operations before and during the early years of the war.

which women could drive and what vehicles they had access to. Those vehicles which could easily be converted into fire tenders or especially ambulances were also listed. This formidable lady was then into her late fifties but pointed out to me that she was younger than Churchill! She set about contacting past and present Girl Guide officers and they helped her to designate what she defined as 'bed spaces' plus potential rest and reception centres. She travelled more than 20,000 miles in her car over a period of eight months. This would be no mean feat these days but cars were then less reliable, petrol stations fewer in number and some of the minor roads were nothing more than cart tracks.

Lady Ashton donated a WVS mobile canteen.

Rachael Kay-Shuttleworth went from meeting to meeting, keeping careful notes as she went, and when evacuation from areas under threat from bombing began in September 1939 the mass movement in Lancashire went so smoothly that she became famous for her cool efficiency. She was invited to attend a conference of the WVS in London. She described how she organised more than 200 rest centres in the North-West and her methods were quickly followed throughout the rest of Britain.

'Wherever I went, I wore the WVS uniform. This not only saved me money but also I did not have to explain why I was speaking in a particular area. I was not on my own because most women considered that they were a military force to be reckoned with.'

One of Rachael's contacts was Lady Ashton of Ashton Hall, near Lancaster who also became prominent in the WVS. Lady Ashton gave a fully equipped mobile canteen and staffed it with WVS ladies who were ready to help in any emergency. Like Gawthorpe, which is now run by the National Trust, Ashton Hall still stands but is now the clubhouse for Lancaster Golf Club.

The rest centres, which Rachael Kay-Shuttleworth identified so clearly throughout Lancashire, were coordinated and also linked with the billeting system. Those arriving at centres were to be sorted out as soon as possible and moved the minimum distance to be billeted in order to take pressure off the roads. It was also essential to move homeless people as soon as possible in order to make room for others coming in from damaged areas. It was pointed out with great firmness that a homeless person was not a refugee who had moved away in defiance of the 'stand firm' order placed on all civilians. Being bombed out was a traumatic experience and those helping the homeless should be trained to provide help and assurance for people facing a variety of personal problems. This would become acute when some members of a family survived whilst others were killed. The *Consolidated Instructions to Invasion Committees* ordered that at least two persons even in the smallest of villages should be trained in this type of counselling.

I had great pleasure in meeting Mrs Davies who remembered these WVS days very well. She was still at work in 2004 at Hilden Mill office which is part of the Oswaldtwistle Mill Shop complex. She will not retire yet because she is only 92! 'I remember the war years very well,' she said, 'and as I throw nothing away I still have the documents allowing me to use my car on official business and I had to paint the bumpers, mudguards and running boards white because of the blackout. I've also got my old tin hat, as well as some happy memories despite the pressure everybody was under.'

It was anticipated that during invasion and the intensive aerial bombardment which would precede it, the civilian defenders would need to provide both skilled and unskilled labour to clear debris from and repair lines of communication. Civilians would also be needed to assist in the construction of military defence

*Mrs Davies – still working at 92 – and (opposite) her wartime car licence
and Civil Defence badge.*

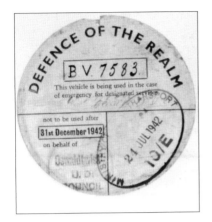 

works and to dig structures such as slit trenches, emergency latrines and common graves.

Registers were kept of all those physically able to carry out these essential manual tasks and some of the local clergy helped to identify such labourers. A distinction was made between these men and others who had other more important jobs to attend to other than grave digging. Retired schoolteachers were also recruited to compile these lists and details available from local employment exchanges were also used.

Defence Regulation 84AA was in force, which designated an Operational Area Defence Officer, to be appointed by the Ministry of Labour and National Service. He could direct all but a few exempted individuals to carry out essential work in repelling the invasion and to maintain all vital services. This order 84AA would take precedence over all other orders.

Ambulances and medical services were also vital. Vehicles were to be commandeered and converted into ambulances, fire appliances or mobile kitchens; those with a large boot and substantial roofs were easily adapted to become ambulances, which were surprisingly well equipped. Mobile fire pumps were also added to privately owned vehicles.

Not only were civilians advised to remain in situ they were also encouraged to keep working. Only in the event of the German

Many private cars were adapted for use should invasion come. The boot housed a mobile first aid post.

invasion being totally successful was there to be any attempt to sabotage equipment. It was very sensible to accept that if an invasion was to be repelled all armament production should be accelerated in order to maintain supply lines to the friendly forces.

The list of police responsibilities seemed endless and they were charged with the control of traffic and ensuring that members of the public 'stood firm' (whatever that meant), while they also had to implement the newly constituted Army Act. This involved the police having the responsibility for billeting soldiers. There also had to be a close and direct liaison between the police and the Invasion Committee.

During an invasion the National Fire Service, in addition to the normal duties, was to be charged with dealing with burning buildings directly on routes of military importance. The fire service had to block enemy movements by actually setting fire to buildings on each side of roads which the Germans could use. These routes were carefully designated as invasion threatened and care had to be taken to balance these activities with the designated 'stand firm' policy.

The fire service also worked closely with the police and the Invasion Committee to produce a list of buildings in a priority

*A member of the Women's Auxiliary Police Corps
on duty in Manchester.*

order to be saved if lots of buildings were on fire at the same time. They were made aware of which buildings were being used as coordination centres. Initially only a senior fire officer and the responsible government official knew which of these buildings was on the priority list; obviously the whereabouts of key buildings should not become public knowledge and therefore vulnerable to potential German informers.

If gas was used by the enemy, specially trained civilian teams were to be brought into force and neutralising chemicals, especially lime, were stockpiled. Blocked roads and debris had to be efficiently removed if friendly forces required quick passage. Mobile fire crews were also trained to react quickly and flexibly with vehicles being quickly requisitioned and adapted.

The Invasion Committees were given definite orders that the normal civilian administration should be continued as long as possible and efforts were made to ensure that responsible army personnel were fully aware of how civil authorities worked, especially relating to police, APR, fire and ambulance services. Joint exercises were held specifically relating to cooperation between towns and cities such as Liverpool and Manchester.

To work efficiently under these conditions and also to continually check identity cards and cope with other legalities the police needed help, but it had to be help they could trust. Ron Ormerod of Brierfield, near Burnley, told me of what became known as the PAMS scheme: 'This stood for the Police Auxiliary Messenger Service and those who volunteered for this were provided with the necessary documentation. This took some of the pressure off the police who had all sorts of things to check and the man on the beat was really under pressure. The PAMS could check identification cards but did not have the power of arrest.' Dennis Wood, working now at the Police Museum in Manchester, has been able, he says 'to read the notebooks of coppers on the beat during the war years. They were helped by Women's Auxiliary Police Corps and these lasses did a part time service in addition to carrying out their normal jobs.'

From German documents captured after the war it was realised

The Alt estuary was one of many places in Lancashire which the Germans had identified as potential 'landing sites'.

that detailed plans and aerial photographs of possible landing areas had been obtained in the mid-1930s. It made total sense therefore to take all these precautions, however remote from the battlefields of Europe they seemed to be.

141

Chapter 10

Repel the Enemy

The German invasions of several countries, especially Poland, had involved intense bombing spearheaded by Stukas, prior to troop movements on the ground. British invasion plans anticipated the enemy bombing of docks, airfields, railways and communication links which would disrupt morale. In the case of the North-West of England, attacks on the Liverpool, Manchester and Barrow docks were sure to take place and associated with this paratroop drops were expected to take defences in the rear. They would certainly have met with stern resistance.

It was also anticipated that the Germans would have plans to mislead or alarm the population. False notices and information would have been prepared beforehand and there was every reason to suppose that agents would have been active for several years, and therefore know their neighbourhood well, as enemy plans had been formulated by the mid 1930s.

In order to make it as difficult as possible to spread misinformation, Regional Commissioners were given powers listed under Defence Regulation 16A. Directions were made that only local notices could be displayed on official notice boards. Nobody could display a notice unless it was officially approved and appropriate checks and balances were put in place to ensure that forgeries were detected. Local people all knew each other in those days and folk were much less mobile than is the case today – cars would be known both by make and by number and the drivers by face and by name. All reports and notices were obliged to be checked and re-checked, while orders given by loudspeaker vans should be checked for authenticity. Every instruction should ideally be checked back to the original source and any messengers known personally to the receiver.

It was considered that the most reliable transportation for messengers would be a pedal cycle and in the case of remote hills, good foot runners were vital. The Lake District and the Lancashire Moors had long had a tradition of hill running with men remaining fit and active until well into their sixties – a few were even older than this. Young lads recruited by the Post Office as messenger boys delivered telegrams, but were also taught to transmit, read and interpret morse code. These lads knew their patch so well that they were on speaking terms with almost everyone in their area.

Plans also had to be made to organise an aggressive reaction to invading troops. In this respect the Home Guard was essential.

On 13th May 1940, just three days after he became Prime Minister, Winston Churchill delivered his now famous speech which included the phrase: 'I have nothing to offer but blood, toil, tears and sweat.' Churchill was not just good with words, he was also very much a man of action. Anthony Eden was appointed as Secretary for War and he announced the formation of the Local Defence Volunteers. This was abbreviated to LDV, which was soon popularly translated as 'Look, Duck and Vanish'. By the end of May, 250,000 men had volunteered and by July that number had doubled and the Volunteers had been renamed the Home Guard.

Would the force see action? France surrendered on 22nd June 1940, after the British Expeditionary Force which had been all but

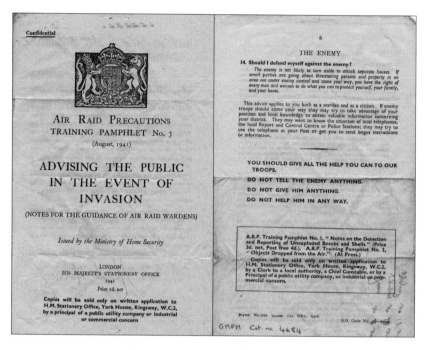

Instructions in case of invasion.

lost was saved at Dunkirk. Most observers felt that the threat of invasion was closer than at any time since the days of Napoleon. Churchill was insisting that the British would fight on the beaches or in the hills, and old weapons in museums or in private collections were oiled and got ready for action. Shotguns and even air rifles were lovingly polished and even wooden replicas and pitchforks were brought into service. All were waiting for the password – *Cromwell* – before gathering in the local Home Guard stations to await orders. In the end the RAF won the Battle of Britain and the invasion was put off, but the Home Guard stayed on duty.

They took on the task of guarding installations and manning coastal defences, thus releasing regular troops for the battlegrounds overseas. In 1943 women were allowed to join the

Home Guard as auxiliaries and although they had no uniforms they were given some weapon training, though they mainly functioned as signallers and clerks. In those days the morse code was vital because radio transmitters were large and heavy and not easily carried.

The television series *Dad's Army* was meant to be funny, and indeed it was, but with an element of truth built into the plots. There is no doubt that if the invasion had come the Home Guard would have suffered heavy losses. The Germans decreed that they were civilians and therefore not subject to the Geneva Convention. Anyone captured would be shot and it would be a capital offence to carry any weapon or a radio transmitter, or to post any unauthorised notice. Furthermore, the Germans intended to send all males between 17 and 65 to camps in France. All these German orders guaranteed that the Home Guard would have resisted. Look, Duck and Vanish into the hills to continue fighting would have been the choice of all the Home Guard survivors.

The concept of the Home Guard as old men and boys fighting with sharpened clothes props and pitchforks was true only in the very early days. They were given a limited supply of weapons used by the regular army but other equipment was provided. There was a significant hard core of very able fighters who would have made life extremely difficult for any invaders, especially for lightly armed paratroops intent only upon establishing bridgeheads.

Few people are aware that the American FBI had a problem which they felt that the British Home Guard could solve. They had a huge arsenal of weapons and ammunition which they had confiscated from the gangsters of the 1930s, so well known to us from Hollywood films. Tommy guns, automatics and other lethal weapons were shipped over in the holds of Lease Lend ships and given to what are best described as Home Guard Special Units. These weapons were hidden under beds but with care taken to store the ammunition in different and secret locations until they were needed.

Then came the invention of the Sten gun, which was a purpose-built weapon specially designed for the Home Guard. Its design

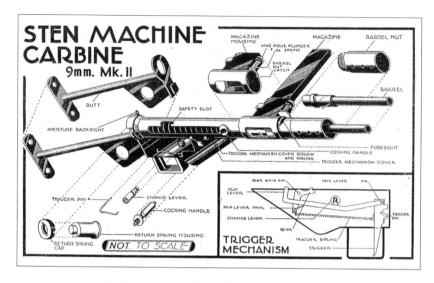

The Sten gun, produced for the Home Guard.

was simple, so it was cheap to produce, and it came complete with an instruction manual. Its official title was a Sten Machine Carbine Mark 2 and it had a 32-round capacity. It could fire all types of 9 millimetre ammunition including that used by the German army, which would have enabled ammunition captured from the invading force to be fired back at them. Sten guns were manufactured in many factories, all kept secret though they included the Hornby/Meccano factories in Liverpool. Production could therefore be guaranteed at a local level and weapons delivered to those groups fighting close to home.

All members of the Home Guard signed and strictly adhered to the Official Secrets Act. Recruits had to know their areas well and ideal members were farmers, postmen, quarry workers, gamekeepers and poachers. The latter two groups worked well together especially in parts of the Lake District.

Whilst plans were made to resist invasion, the next move would have been to 'push the invaders back into the sea'. Initially, however, any troops landing by sea were to be slowed down and

146

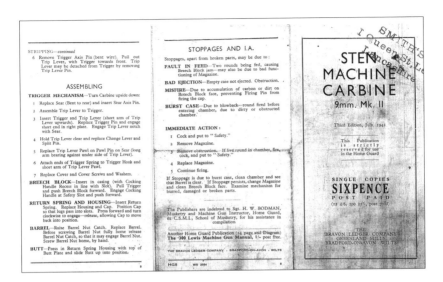

Sten gun manual.

the more efficiently this was done the more effective the contingency plans would be.

The large harbours around Liverpool and to a lesser extent Barrow-in-Furness would be well protected but the smaller, but still flat, sandy beaches also had to be defended. These were to be strewn with blocks of concrete, networks of barbed wire and other obstructions including gun emplacements and pillboxes. There was also a degree of bluff in this, as Ted Cowlishaw told me: 'As a postman I noticed lots of guns set in the sand dunes between Barrow and Askam. A close look revealed that most of these so-called "guns" were actually telegraph poles set at an aggressive angle and painted to look very realistic.'

Pillboxes were built and gun emplacements were concentrated among the sand dunes. At the South Walney Bird Reserve run by the Cumbria Naturalists Trust these concrete emplacements now function as excellent but unofficial bird hides. Other remnants are still apparent on the coastal path around the village of Pilling set near the Wyre estuary.

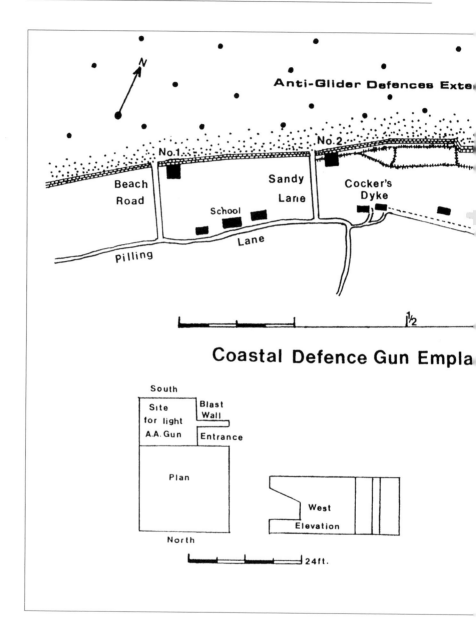

Coastal defence gun emplacements at Pilling in 1940.

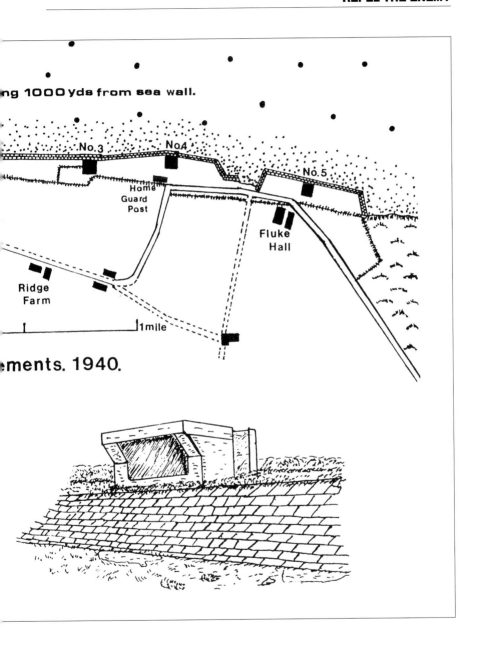

ng 1000 yds from sea wall.

No.3   No.4

No.5

Home
Guard
Post

Fluke
Hall

Ridge
Farm

1 mile

ments. 1940.

The next estuary to the south is that of the Lune which is guarded by two harbours: Sunderland Point and Glasson Dock. From Roman times until the 18th century, Lancaster was an important harbour but a combination of the silting up of the River Lune and the construction of larger ships meant that other ports were built at the estuary mouth.

Sunderland itself was redundant as a port by the late 18th century but its flat sands would certainly have been attractive to invading forces, especially if the Germans came from Southern Ireland. Looked at with hindsight this seems unlikely but in 1940 the threat was real and plans had to be made. This involved the production of huge volumes of cement. Also vital were supplies of timber. At Sunderland Point, for example, large numbers of wooden posts were embedded apparently haphazardly in the mud and sand banks. By late 1939 the Army were already present at the north end of the village and their Nissen huts were inhabited. Still there, buried ever deeper in the sands, are the huge concrete blocks designed to prevent or delay the movement of armoured vehicles and all but the largest of tanks.

Sunderland is a remote spot even today and the causeway leading to it is covered by the tide twice every day. It still presents an impossible-to-breach barrier between Sunderland Point on one side and the little village of Overton on the other.

The responsibility of the Army was to man the anti-aircraft battery as well as to keep an eye on movement of enemy aircraft with the help of the Royal Observer Corps. On the opposite side of the Lune estuary is Glasson Dock, which still functions today as a minor port. In the 1940s there was a railway link between Glasson and the town of Lancaster. This had a courtesy stop at Ashton Hall but was closed in the 1960s. It is now a footpath and linear nature reserve.

Not only the Germans, but also the Regional Invasion Committees looked closely at the flat sandy areas, including a huge expanse of open beach at Pilling. A sea wall was constructed along Pilling Lane and as part of this wall five gun emplacements were constructed. These were never permanently occupied by

Gun emplacements in Pilling.

troops and no guns were placed there. They were, however, ready for occupation and the local Home Guard used them as observation posts. Large numbers of poles were embedded in the sands to deter landing craft, or more likely gliders, coming in to bring troops. Inland of the sea wall, gun emplacements and anti-aircraft gun supports were built. What would have happened was that 4.7-inch naval guns similar to those in position to guard the Port of Fleetwood would have been made available had the German plans materialised. Over the years since the war the sea wall has been strengthened on several occasions and these works have obscured the gun emplacements, but those with an observant turn of mind can still see them and gain some idea of their strength.

Communications were a problem at this time and the construction of a new telephone exchange at Pilling in 1937 may or may not have been a coincidence. It continued to operate until 1967 and has been incorporated into the museum which is part of the Farmer Parr's visitors' centre at Fleetwood.

Lighthouses around the North-West coastline made good

Pilling telephone exchange, preserved as a museum.

observation posts for firewatchers, Home Guard and the Royal Observer Corps. This applied to several lighthouses which were already redundant, or at best of limited use and included those at Hale on the Mersey, on Cockerham Sands and at Walney Island. The monument on top of Hoad Hill above Ulverston was also useful – it was built as a replica of the Eddyston lighthouse to celebrate the life of Sir John Barrow (1764–1848) who was born in the town; he was Secretary of the Admiralty and he wrote the official account of the Mutiny on the Bounty. This still stands proudly over the town.

The lighthouse on Walney Island near Barrow-in-Furness also survives. It was built in 1790 to guide ships from the West Indies into Lancaster docks, long before Barrow had a harbour of its own. During the war there was a substantial coastal defence battery with up to 200 troops in residence. The lighthouse was the officers' mess and the remnants of the barracks for the troops also remain. As the invasion threat receded German prisoners of war were housed on the site. It is still possible to see gun emplacements among the dunes and also a substantial structure called the Fort, which the soldiers used as a defensive focus, though this is now showing signs of wear and tear.

In Lancashire there were other towers situated inland which proved to be excellent observation points, including Darwen Tower and the Peel Monument. Both these towers had panoramic views and overlooked vital industrial areas and especially busy railway lines.

Darwen Tower, also known as Jubilee Tower, was built in 1897 and it was a place from which most of East Lancashire could be seen. Here then was the perfect place for firewatchers and members of the Royal Observer Corps. Slit trenches were cut into the soft peaty ground of the moorland. The same applied to the Peel Tower, set high on the hills between Rawtenstall and Bury. From the tower, built in the 1850s to celebrate the life of Prime Minister and local lad Sir Robert Peel who founded the police force, the whole of the Irwell Valley could be seen including road, rail and canal routes.

Chapter 11

A Secret Army – Fact or Fiction?

The question is often asked – was there a secret army ready to fight if a German invasion was successful and enemy troops either landed by sea or were dropped from the air? The answer would seem to be yes, there was. And although many of the details remain undisclosed to this day and, indeed, most of the people involved are now dead and their secrets have been buried with them, it is possible to piece together the Resistance movement that would have emerged here in Lancashire.

The Boy Scout motto of 'Be Prepared' was taken seriously in the Britain of 1940. There was a British government incentive to set up a 'secret army', as they were disappointed that the German army had marched through France with so little opposition. Only later did the French civilians set up an organised resistance.

Military intelligence therefore created what became known as Auxiliary Units which operated under the cover of the Home Guard. Experienced old army officers, often in their eighties, set about recruiting young men who knew their local countryside. A booklet was produced, the cover proclaiming it to be *The*

Countryman's Diary but which was in fact a sort of future SAS logbook. Under great secrecy this was distributed to a few reliable people and contained instructions on killing the enemy and sabotaging equipment and communications.

Targeted for inclusion in this Resistance army were anglers, poachers, quarrymen, miners, foresters, postmen, gamekeepers and others. All were sworn to secrecy, they were never called up and even wives and mothers did not know what they were up to. Many were taunted as cowards and even attacked by servicemen on leave. They were, however, told always to keep out of trouble and not react to any sort of provocation.

Working at night, they prepared hides and built underground burrows often the size of Nissen huts, while long forgotten caves and old mine shafts were secretly reopened. In some cases huts were actually buried underground. In Lancashire and the Lake District there was no shortage of these hideouts and I have seen evidence of such refuges at Coniston copper mines and the coal mines around Wigan and Bacup, but even now getting the few old-timers left to talk about these plans is often like trying to get blood out of a stone.

Each unit was provided with a ten-day supply of food and water after which they were expected to live off the land. This would have been no problem, as Will Renson told me:

> I had been poaching since I was ten and could trap rabbits, tickle trout and net salmon without any problem. It was fun working in a team with John Brocklebank, the gamekeeper who had taken me to court on several occasions but he never had enough evidence to jail me. It was the local magistrate and landowner who had been a captain in the First World War who recruited us both.

The Home Guard inaugurated three battalions in Britain which were a cover for these Auxiliary Units. The 201st unit was to operate in Scotland, the 202nd unit in Northern England, whilst the 203rd were based in the South. No list of the men recruited was

155

ever made and the ordinary members of the Home Guard would either not have known about the units or would have denied all knowledge of them. Even to this day some of their material is officially classified as secret.

Many of the underground hideouts were constructed close to stately homes or large houses with extensive grounds. Quite rightly, it was assumed that German commanders would take over these estates for themselves as had happened in France. The units would then be close by and therefore able to kill these high-ranking officers or at least disrupt their communications.

Before these units were set up the landowners would have been carefully monitored to discover if they had any fascist sympathies – if so they would have themselves been the subject of early attacks from the units. Sir Oswald Mosley's estates were in Manchester and some of his friends may well have had fascist leanings. On the whole, however, the large estates would have been ideal areas from which the units could operate.

Some rich landowners were involved in plans, which they often funded themselves in order to preserve secrecy, to set up resistance cells in the event of a successful German invasion. Roger Fleetwood-Hesketh of Meols Hall at Churchtown, near Southport, was one such. Born in 1902, he held a commission in the Lancashire yeomanry in 1922, after being educated at Eton and Christ Church. He was an outspoken critic of Hitler from the early 1930s.

Not only was Fleetwood-Hesketh rich but he was also very intelligent and there is plenty of evidence to suggest that had the Germans invaded he already had plans afoot to resist their troops very efficiently indeed. Once the invasion threat receded Fleetwood-Hesketh did not disband his private army but turned some of his attention towards the Allied invasion of Europe. He conceived and ran what became known as Operation Fortitude prior to D-Day (see chapter 6), when he successfully persuaded the German High Command that the invasion would come via Boulogne and Calais. Fleetwood-Hesketh used a series of double agents (some trained at Ringway) who were parachuted into

Meols Hall, home of Roger Fleetwood-Hesketh.

German-occupied Europe, and he also used spoof radio and radar communications which helped to cause further confusion.

If this man could confuse the Germans so completely prior to Normandy he would have been a most formidable opponent if the enemy had successfully landed on the Lancashire coast. Fleetwood-Hesketh built up a nucleus of local men he could trust. One was Alan Potts of Southport, who was then only 18 but had great artistic talent. Later he worked with Fleetwood-Hesketh on the secret maps compiled during the build up to the invasion of Europe in 1944.

Roger Fleetwood-Hesketh was far removed from an eccentric but there was one character who would certainly have been defined as such. He was Major Armstrong, well known for his books on big game hunting throughout the world. He trained a group of Home Guard lads in the art of unarmed combat, marksmanship and camouflage. Peter Ainsworth who still lives in Chorley was one of the Armstrong brigade:

Peter Ainsworth of Chorley.

We were trained in the grounds of Worden Hall near Leyland but we travelled all over with the Major to demonstrate our military skills under his direction. At first we felt stupid blacking our faces and weaving vegetation into our uniform until we saw some of our members walking away from us and then blending so well into the landscape that they seemed to disappear. We learned to crawl properly and shoot straight. I think it was in 1942 that the government sponsored a book written by Major Armstrong about his tactics. This was called *Fieldcraft and Stealth*.

In the event of a German landing, marksmen from these units operating from deep cover would have inflicted major casualties. Many of the men learned their skills at the Altcar Rifle Range, situated on the sand dunes of the Alt estuary, a river second only to the Mersey in the importance of Liverpool, and which was described in chapter 7. I was privileged to be given a guided tour of this site by Major Bill Hunter, the Commandant of the Territorial Army unit at Altcar. The remains of the massive anti-aircraft gun emplacements which gave protection to the docklands as enemy bombers attempted to cause massive disruption are still standing, and still in use are the Nissen huts used by regular troops and Home Guard during the war. If an invasion had succeeded then the Altcar training camp would have played a vital role. Major Hunter also showed me heavier weapons which were collected during the war – if the need arose these would have 'disappeared' along with substantial quantities of ammunition – and manuals relating to German weapons so that captured supplies could have been turned on the enemy.

Further along these sand dunes from Altcar was Fort Crosby. This was a substantial gun battery situated between Hightown and Hall Road railway stations. Fort Crosby had several military planning rooms and a number of ammunition dumps located deep underground. The 'Fort' had its own railway halt which was named Sniggery Crossing. It was no small or insignificant part of

Major Armstrong's Brigade.

Major Armstrong's Brigade in action.

Altcar Second World War buildings, photographed in 2005.

Liverpool's defences. It even had its own sports facilities and hospital, although it was well disguised so that it did not look so formidable. Once the threat of invasion had faded the Fort was adapted and more than 1,000 German prisoners of war were accommodated at the camp. The Territorial Army used Fort Crosby until 1954 and in 1967 the place was blown up with only a few stones now remaining. It would, however, have been a formidable base for the initial defences resisting invading forces.

The worst possible scenario would have been for these facilities to have been overrun. Churchill's words would, however, still have been heeded. After fighting on the beaches and in the streets, the resistance would have continued into the hills of the North-West.

All fighting units need to be able to operate independently but it is always essential to be able to communicate. They would have known where field telephones were located, some dating to the First World War, but as war became a certainty many young people including Scout and Guide troops were trained to use semaphore and have a working knowledge of the morse code.

If all electronic or visual lines of communication should be broken then homing pigeons would be used. Even on the beaches of Normandy some newspaper war correspondents used pigeons to get their stories home when all available lines were being used by the military.

The North-West of England had long been a haven for pigeon fanciers, mainly miners and cotton workers needing an excuse to be out in the fresh air during their few hours of leisure. Many lived for their pigeons and their allotments, both of which provided food during and just after the war years. Pigeon racing was also a competitive sport and an enjoyable way of risking a few hard earned shillings by betting on results.

The concept of using homing pigeons if the Germans invaded was apparently inspired by the police in Lancashire. During the Liverpool blitz of 1940 all telephone links with the city had been

The wartime Nissen huts, still used at Altcar.

Fort Crosby, photographed in 1949. It was demolished in the 1960s.

disrupted. A pigeon was despatched carrying a message describing the damage to Seaforth docks and asking for extra fire appliances and other Civil Defence workers. The pigeon arrived at the police HQ at Hutton near Preston two hours before the telephones and other networks were partially restored.

This gave the impetus to establish the Lancashire Constabulary Voluntary Pigeon Service, with the encouragement of Chief Constable Archie Horden who had served as an army captain during the First World War. He gave the organising brief to Neil Galbraith, later Chief Constable in North Wales, who recalls:

At the start of the war everybody who kept pigeons needed a licence. The initial idea was that these must not fall into the hands of any invading forces but should be used by resistance fighters. I was the sergeant who had to issue the permits so I was the obvious choice when it came to organising the Pigeon Service. This was not so daft as it sounds because the army and the RAF had their own pigeon service but it was not well organised. Airmen, in particular, had enough to do escaping from stricken aircraft without writing a message giving their exact position before crashing! The pigeon fanciers of Lancashire were over the moon not just to 'fight' for their King and Country but the new system also allowed them to purchase more bird food which was also rationed during the war. This enabled them to keep their favourite birds alive during this period.

According to Eric Hardy, the founder of *Wild Birds* magazine and a Liverpool man who served with the pigeon service during the war, 28 pigeons were awarded the Dickin Medal between 1941 and 1945. Some birds were released from aircraft which were being shot down whilst others sent messages from Arnhem and from the Normandy beaches.

It is interesting that Eric Hardy was also an expert on the distribution of birds of prey, especially in the North-West of England. Peregrines still breed on the top of some of Liverpool's warehouses and on the huge Indian mill chimney overlooking the town of Darwen, as well as around the West Pennine Moors.

There has been some controversy in recent years regarding the threat caused by peregrine falcons to valuable racing pigeons. Equally controversial was the contention that peregrine falcons and their nests would have been targeted if Britain was invaded by the Germans, and there have been suggestions that no plans were made to put this into practice. In 1999, however, previously secret information was released showing that Britain had a team of specially trained falconers. Their function, or rather their birds' function, was to counter known German spies sending information out of Britain by carrier pigeon. These detailed records are now kept in The National Archives at Kew.

It goes without saying that if Britain was invaded and radio messages were being intercepted or their operators being tracked by the German occupying forces then pigeons might be an answer – and birds of prey might then be a danger to our own forces.

For the last 40 years I have lived on the Lancashire-Yorkshire border and have spoken to many old miners about pigeons and peregrines. In the 1960s I was friendly with John Nuttall. John was a miner from Burnley and a renowned ornithologist and expert on ringing of birds. We often spoke about peregrines and he knew that in the early years of the war peregrine nest sites in the West

Old salt mines not flooded at Preesall, near Fleetwood, could have provided hideouts.

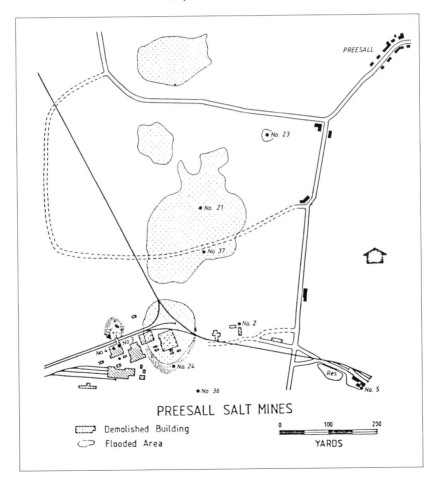

PREESALL SALT MINES

Demolished Building

Flooded Area

YARDS

Pennine Moors and also around the Trough of Bowland were mapped. My father also told me that it was important during the war to map the nests of the peregrine falcons in the Lake District. He began work as a post office telegrapher who specialised in teaching servicemen the art of the morse code and was based first at Millom and then in Lincolnshire. The mapping of peregrines was another aspect which he told me was his hobby. I often wonder if it was also work related.

Resistance forces needed not only good communications but also to be able to move quickly without relying on petrol-driven vehicles. In all country districts there were those skilled in horse riding and during the war many were specially trained to ride horses and ponies over rough country. Some Home Guard units were taught to ride using not only proper saddles but also bare back, as was the case with some units in Lancashire, Cumberland and Westmorland.

Explosives experts were also urgently recruited, many too old to be called up but some placed in 'specially protected' categories. From the earliest days lead, copper and coal miners were well used to keeping their powder dry. Miners traditionally worked in teams led by a self-appointed captain and they were paid by the weight of ore which they produced. They had to pay for their own tools, candles and gunpowder and so they learned to keep the locations of these supplies very secret. Any occupying force would have found this collective experience very difficult to handle, especially when small groups of men disappeared literally into the bowels of the earth. There were hundreds of disused small coal mines throughout Lancashire and these would have been impossible for the Germans to locate. During the war many young men were called up to work in coal mines rather than the armed forces and a few of these 'Bevin Boys' were specially trained to plan what was literally an underground movement.

Quarry workers would also have had skills useful during any resistance movement. In the Lake District the slate workers were a good recruiting ground for these specialist units. Although well past his first flush of youth at the start of the war, Bert Fryer was

This mounted unit of the Home Guard, in what is now Cumbria, could operate without saddles!

one such. A famous and sometimes a 'difficult' sportsman to compete against, he was a football referee well known to my father and a cricket umpire well known to myself and others when we were learning the game. Bert Fryer, however, knew slate, he knew explosives and he was an excellent fell runner who had won many cash prizes. He knew his local hills better than any man I have ever met and even the most formidable of German troops would have found Bert hard to handle. Bert often came across Harry Burton who was the blacksmith at Broughton-in-Furness. Harry was strong, fit, fiercely independent and a cricketing legend who cursed umpires, especially Bert Fryer. Harry could, as they said in Broughton, 'mek owt out of iron' and he and Bert were 'loosely associated during the war'. Things would have tightened if the Germans had landed.

It is known that important communication links were identified and at the last moment 'skilled units' would have blown up

Old shafts of coal mines, such as this one at Old Meadows near Bacup,
although long disused, would have been valuable hideouts
following a German invasion.